City Priest, City People

City Priest, City People
One Man's Journal, Book 2

Herbert O'Driscoll

Anglican Book Centre
Toronto, Ontario

1983
Anglican Book Centre
600 Jarvis Street
Toronto, Ontario
Canada M4Y 2J6

Printed in Canada

Canadian Cataloguing in Publication Data

O'Driscoll, Herbert, 1928-
  One man's journal

Vol. 2 has title: City priest, city people.
ISBN 0-919030-89-0 (v.1). - ISBN 0-919891-04-7 (v.2)

1. O'Driscoll, Herbert, 1928- 2. Anglican Church
of Canada - Clergy - Biography. I. One man's
journal (Radio Program). II. Title. III. Title: City
priest, city people.

BX5620.037A3 1982   283'.092'4   C83-004970-3

*for Alan
and Esther
in long friendship*

Contents

The City

We may live away from the city itself, but to be within sound of a radio or within sight of a television screen, or to see a weather station on a nearby mountain top or the winking light of a jet-liner — all these things make us to some extent city folk. There are very few *rural* men and women in the true sense of that word.

For all our long-time dwelling in cities we are not yet fully reconciled to the city being the natural habitat of faith. Deep down we feel the city is essentially human rather than divine. We betray this in many ways. Hardly a Christian hymn refers to the city in other than negative terms. We have never fully acknowledged that the Bible ends in a Holy City. We wax much more eloquent about churches in green fields and villages than about churches crouched at the bottom of canyons of gleaming glass and steel. City churches, especially downtown churches, are rather like Dr Johnson's famous dog who stood on its hindlegs. For many the wonder is not that city churches often have a fascinatingly varied life but that they have any life at all!

Priesthood of course is priesthood wherever it is practiced. If there is a difference downtown, it is that much of one's life there is spent moving in the urban milieu immediately outside the door. In the suburbs or in the countryside the church door opens on what is for the most part familiar and predictable. To open such doors is to look out on something immediately thought of as "the parish," to see a familiar face passing, to wave to a child, to look at a house where such-and-such a family lives. Here ministry can be rich and at times demanding.

Downtown the pretence that only the surrounding area is the parish, in any intimate and possessed way, is impossible. There are of course familiar faces; there are smiles exchanged and salutations. But, except for occasional meetings with actual members of the congregation, such encounters are light brushes in acquaintance. When the door of a downtown church opens, it can be anybody in any kind of mood and with any kind of intent or none, needing a hand-out or advice or reassurance or forgiveness, sometimes for real and sometimes for imagined sins. Downtown encounters require instant and instinctive assessing of where the other person is in their inner world. Such encounters can mean calming fears, listening to confused minds, refusing pointless and unwise hand-outs, absorbing anger.

Much of one's work downtown is of course in the places in which any priest's work is done, in a hospital ward, in an apartment. But it is done too in the convention rooms of nearby hotels, in radio station booths, in television interviews, in universities or community colleges, in courtrooms, in business offices, in clubs.

To look at the roster of names of a suburban or rural church is for the most part to see traditional patterns of life, families, older couples, individuals. Downtown the mosaic is richer, the families of mother and father and the children are there, but they are fewer. There will be a greater number of single parents. There will be more individuals, many with fragile and irregular lives. There will be people of long tradition who, either by sheer resilience or great openness or fantastic innocence, are impervious to the shocks of the cosmopolitanism around them, bringing to it all a sweetness and gentleness that sometimes hides their quiet awareness and wisdom. All these people together form a rich and subtle mingling of needs and gifts.

Among them, and by the ministry of all of them, urban ministry is carried on. At the heart of it all, uniting it with all other ministry, is the altar in the city where the Word is read and proclaimed and the eternal sacrifice is offered. Whether it be within or beyond history, that sacrifice and that Word will bring to pass in our all too human city that glory envisioned by the apostle John and named the Holy City.

Home

Human Dignity

I think I find myself coming across the word *dignity* more than I used to. We are beginning to use it frequently in the great discussion, going on all around the world, about how we make decisions in medicine regarding the means we choose to prolong or end life. We are more and more saying that at a certain stage a person should be left with their dignity, rather than be subjected to procedures that continue life at the cost of that same dignity.

I thought of this again recently in another kind of situation. We will call him Frank. It isn't his name, but it will do. Frank has lived for a number of years in a single room downtown in a building generously defined as a hotel. He is very old now and getting very feeble. But in this particular place Frank is very content. He eats a meal in a nearby restaurant. People know him and like him. He is saluted on the street on his short slow walks. There are a few places where he is known by name when, for instance, he buys a few groceries. In a word, Frank is in that particular area at *home*.

But Frank is feeble, and it is reasonable to question whether he can be left alone in safety. Twice now he has been gently persuaded to give up the room. Each time he has gone to a very pleasant place where he has been cared for and given his meals. He has also been able to go out from that place when he wishes. But twice Frank has found it impossible to live in that place, and he has left and gone back to his downtown room.

Outside of his window there is the sound of the next block being transformed into a highrise. Along the narrow corridor outside his room there are constant noises. Sometimes they are the unpleasant and even frightening sounds of argument. Negotiating the street is becoming a problem. Some day a mat will slip, a step on the stairs won't be there, somebody will cut the corner on a yellow light. Someday anything may happen.

But perhaps that's the way it has to be. Because one of the things that Frank has a right to keep is that very ability to choose. He has a right to choose contentment as he sees it. He has a right to the way he wants to live and maybe the way he wishes to die. If you are Frank's priest, it gives you long, long thoughts. But I think that it is part of what keeping his dignity means.

Jesus said . . . when you were young, you girded yourself and walked where you would; but when you are old . . . another will gird you and carry you where you do not wish to go. John 21:18

A Misplaced Kindness

I remember once reading in some article, or it may have been listening to a speaker, that among the most annoying experiences of old age is to be patronized. We are often given to treating an elderly person in much the same way as we treat a child. Our voices take on another tone. We are solicitous. We become in the most obvious way helpful. We develop innocuous smiles. We say endlessly nice things. Sometimes, if our contemporaries are present, we punctuate our communications to the elderly with knowing glances which say that we are doing our best in a difficult situation. We are being kind.

We often walk away from such conversations completely oblivious of what is really passing through the mind of that elderly person. We forget that nine times out of ten a long experience of life and relationships and character have enabled them to be perfectly aware, within ten seconds of meeting us, of what exactly our attitude to them is. Sometimes they become so resigned to this approach that they give up fighting it and just play along.

I was reminded of this myself not long ago. I had been asked to pick her up at her apartment block because someone else's car had broken down. Because she was quite elderly I too fell into that trap of being over solicitous. The weather as a subject was handy to begin with. Perhaps then there was some inane remark about this and that and whatever. But as the minutes passed, I slowly began to realize that a very alive and brilliant mind was sitting beside me, the kind of mind who, it turned out, was capable not just of responding to the mention of the name Teilhard de Chardin, but had read more than I ever had of all that he had written, and in the original French!

Since then I have been amused when I notice others adopting the same "help a nice old lady or gentlemen" stance as I once did.

Honour your father and your mother . . . . Exodus 20:12

A Door Opening

Every day all over this and many other cities, scores of ovens are turned on in the morning. They are not turned on for the patrons of large hotels or for families. Into them are placed thousands of meals for a huge army of people who await them. When they are ready, the meals go into scores if not hundreds of cars and then to single dwelling basements, lonely rooms, highrise apartments — in fact, every kind of human dwelling. In different cities there are different names for this kind of program. It is a quiet and very effective service which has been going on for years, thanks to hundreds of volunteers.

I thought of them all the other day when one of them told me a simple and yet very moving story. The person who told me this incident spoke of watching a wonderful thing happen to another human being. One of the people on the beat assigned to her turned out to be in a rather special situation. She lived alone; the apartment was dusty and untidy; she was dishevelled, hair awry, careless of her appearance. Then there came the idea of meals being sent in. It had been suggested by a social worker.

My friend was assigned to her, and each day she began to call with a meal. As she did so, she noticed an interesting thing beginning to happen. After a couple of weeks, the room began to be tidied. Then the elderly occupant began to come to the door more and more pleasantly dressed, more and more well groomed, walking more and more sprightly, talking more and more. Within a month or so, person and apartment were totally transformed. When this was sensitively remarked upon, the answer came back, "Well, you see, I had nobody to dust and tidy and dress up for, and now I do."

Interesting to think of all the solitary lives and rooms that would be transformed if there could be one regular caller to dust and tidy and dress up for.

Behold, I stand at the door and knock; if any one hears my voice and opens the door, I will come in to him and eat with him, and he with me. Revelation 3:20

The Ensemble

Late in the evening I was twiddling my way around the dial of the television set. You know how sometimes you search for something suitably mindless, precisely because you want to switch your own mind off after it has been very active. On my way around the uniformly frantic alternative worlds of the many channels, I got a fleeting glimpse of a man's head bent over a musical instrument. On a whim I went back to him, and there I stayed.

What I had come upon was a group playing chamber music. It was, I learned later, the very brilliant Itzak Perlman chamber group. They were playing Bach's Sonata in C Major.

What held me, and it held me to the end, was something I have never quite realized before, at least not with such clarity. Put simply, I suddenly was made aware of the cost of what I was hearing, the cost of beauty, the cost of great art.

The fleeting glimpse that had drawn me was repeated many times. I saw the richness and intensity of the body movements as each player sought for the deep heart of what was being played. Heads were bent and raised, faces tensed and relaxed, jaw muscles rippled, elbows rose and fell. Each player was a hunter stalking the most elusive thing in the world; each was in pursuit of the Holy Grail. When the camera drew back and showed them as a group, they seemed not to be individuals but a single heaving and rippling life form engaged in bringing something to birth, experiencing in the process both the ecstasy and the cost of being agents in the endless activity of divine creation.

Let everything that breathes praise the Lord! Psalm 150: 6

Looking Up

We were chatting about the demands that life makes. There had been for the whole family a move from the east. That always has some costs. Friendships come to an end, at least they cannot be enjoyed as frequently. A new job affects family life. The familiar outlines of work and school and church, shopping and recreation, all have to be found again. There are times when the new life and the new faces, the new neighbourhood itself, are exciting and interesting. There are times when familiar voices and familiar streets and a familiar group are longed for with a kind of ache.

All this we talked about. We went on to talk about the way one goes about living life with its strains and its joys. At one stage we talked about how very powerful a simple thing can be in communicating to us. She said that from the kitchen window she could see small Air West planes as they climb over the Lions Gate Bridge, turn slowly over the gulf, and head toward the island. Sometimes they fly in sunlight and sometimes against the grey mass of clouds on the mountains. For one person they have become a simple everyday symbol of all that calls her upward in life, in the face of that which would crush and drag her down.

From time immemorial, men and women have looked up for grace. We can sneer at that and say how meaningless such concepts as "up" are. Yet its power remains. We know that God is not "up" or "down," but in looking up we acknowledge that we seek a reality above us, in the sense of it being greater than us. To look up is to acknowledge that there exists that which transcends our humanity. Simple though that may be as a thought, it is immensely powerful as a resource for living.

Jesus said: . . . when these things begin to take place, look up and raise your heads, because your redemption is drawing near.
Luke 21: 28

Intimations of Eternity

There is something we all experience that is very difficult to describe. It has to do with the maddeningly elusive quality that I will call completion. Years ago Geoffrey Studdert-Kennedy began a short poem with the lines

Lord,
there is not one thing done.
There is no battle of my life
that I have really won.

There it is, the feeling that we are never going to get it together, never going to catch up, never going to gather up all those maddeningly trivial things that make up everyday existence. In fact, the more we try, the more unfinished the agenda appears. The more assiduously we answer mail, the more return mail we create! I know that I shall never fully organize the millions of transparencies lying in boxes in my house, never return every book lent to me, never have all my bills paid. Need I continue the list?

One more thing. At a lunatic level consider this. For my sins I possess two ancient cars, one with well over 100,000 miles and the other with 90,000 miles travelled. One of my very modest, yet forever unfulfilled, ambitions is to have every bulb at both ends of both cars working. But there seems to be an iron law in the universe, or a demonic fate, that makes this modest ambition impossible to fulfill.

Even now I find myself half joking about it. Yet silly though it sounds, it communicates something important behind the seeming idiocy of it all. It gives me a tantalizing hint about the reality of my situation as a human being. Is it not just possible that the ever present sense of incompletion in my life points to the possibility that life itself is incomplete? If that is so, then the inability to complete a host of silly insubstantial things in daily life points to the possibility that the completion of many great and substantial things lies elsewhere. In other words, is it possible that among these trivialities is hidden an intimation of eternity?

. . . people who speak thus make it clear that they are seeking a homeland. Hebrews 11:14

Seeing and Perceiving

A few days ago I took one of the family to where she is taking courses toward an eventual profession. For various reasons, rain and traffic and so on, I stopped at a certain place in the university complex to let her out. As she walked away from the car, I remained to watch her for a few minutes.

Nothing could be more normal. You have had the same experience with a family member or with a friend. Yet you too have experienced such moments when you have found you were not just idly looking at a person very dear to you. You found yourself doing much more than that. You found yourself really seeing them.

With our children, even after they have ceased actually to be children, this can so easily happen. When they were small children, it tended to happen while they were asleep and one could look down at them. In sleep the face is particularly revealed, the mask even of early years is off. But later in life there are precious moments when there is a seeing of a very dear person, and that seeing is much more than just a looking at them.

What happens in such a moment? It seems to me that there is a dimming of everything else around the other person. That morning as I looked at my child, it seemed to me that buildings, cars, the rain, all faded a little, remaining, if at all, only as background. My child then walked from me into the distance as if she were walking into the heart of a living portrait.

In that moment I was conscious of her being part of myself, carrying in her my strengths and weaknesses, my gifts and poverty, carrying them yet bringing to all of them the factor of the new being she herself is. I was conscious of her total uniqueness as a human being, indeed of the uniqueness of all human beings. It was a moment of mystery. I turned the car and went back into the morning traffic.

The light of the eyes rejoices the heart . . . . Proverbs 15: 30

The Polling Station

It is one of those totally taken for granted things in life. I am going to vote. What could be more normal, more ordinary? I have left voting until I am driving to a nearby hospital. When I arrive at the school where polling is to take place, there are a lot of cars, many people coming and going, crouching against the rain. Because it is just school closing time, there are a number of children around, small hands grasping for adults' hands.

A peaceful scene, intimate and domestic. It's surely not to be taken for granted. There are societies that have not yet known such peace for more than a generation. There are societies that have never known this quiet process.

I go past the school classroom into the gymnasium, turning toward the semi-circle of faces waiting behind the poll tables. These men and women are my neighbours. Nowhere in sight is there a uniform, any symbol of watchfulness or intimidation. Ordinariness? Of course not! The majority of the world today would find such absence of coercion incomprehensible.

I take my voting ballot and move toward the booth. I notice it is made of cardboard. Last time I recall it being made at least of rough wood. It's a silly thought, but I find myself seeing a symbol in that, a symbol of the increasing fragility of a free way of life, fragile partly because we can so easily take it for granted that freedom demands no cost, no commitment, no discipline. The cardboard worries me because I want this booth to be here when my children come to make their free choices in their country.

Unless the Lord watches over the city, the watchman stays awake in vain. Psalm 127:1

An Older Story

I remember one day in school realizing something that came rather like a revelation. You will remember how in some school atlases there will sometimes be, on opposite sides of the book, two maps of a country. One will be a political map showing borders, divisions, roads, provinces — all that kind of thing. The other will be a physical map. All the marks and divisions, all the political and social symbols are gone. There are only the greens and browns and blues of plain and mountain and lake and sea.

I recall realizing once that one map constantly changes and one always, at least for millions of years, remains the same. I recall the moment I discovered that as a boy. I suppose it was at that very moment that I realized the transience of human habitation and human systems.

The other day I had cause to realize that again. I was walking past a noticeboard. On it, announcing a program about Native affairs, there was a map of this part of the world I call home. The map looked the right shape, but it was divided in an entirely unfamiliar way. The divisions were not precise, but certain areas were indicated. All over it were names that were only half familiar. Recited in succession they had a beauty, a kind of verbal music I had never realized before. It was rather like one of those mythical maps in books such as *The Lord of the Rings* or C.S. Lewis's *Kingdom of Narnia*. The names were these — Salish and Tlingit, Kwakuitl and Bella Coola, Haida, Simshian, Athapaskan.

You have guessed of course what I was looking at. I was seeing this coast and these mountains and valleys before any white traveller discovered the rivers and passes through the mountains. This was a time before James Cook's sails were furled in Nootka Sound. I was forming on my lips names that spelt home to people a thousand years before we gave it other names and other boundaries. And when we, in our arrogant ways, speak of our land being "discovered" in the mere yesterday that is the nineteenth century, there are lips and eyes among us who can be excused if they smile.

. . . others have laboured, and you have entered into their labour.
John 4:38

Real and Unreal

I notice a new paperback edition of *The Hero with a Thousand Faces*. I remember the very first time I saw the book. Somebody gave it to me, and I was hooked. I had discovered Joseph Campbell, perhaps one of the most fascinating of all mythologists.

For centuries in high civilizations like the Greeks and the Romans and the Jews, myths were told, sometimes in prose, sometimes in poetry, in drama. Everybody learnt them and took meanings from them. Along with those myths men and women paid attention to dreams.

Something happened to all that process as western society developed. We began to feel that there was what we like to call the "real" world, the world of thinking and creating and making, a rational world. And there was another world, we allowed. It was in some sense unreal, at least less real. We tended to see it as dark and shadowed, of no practical use, somewhat dangerous, and certainly not worth a great deal of serious attention. Into that category went myths and dreams. Myths actually survived because they were thought to be acceptable for children, and so they were passed on as stories. We have used that word *stories* for centuries in a patronizing and superior way.

Not very long ago as history goes, two men, each in his own way, changed all that attitude. One was Sigmund Freud and the other was Carl Jung. These two, although very different in their stances and in their beliefs, gave us back the world of myths and dreams. They said that we should be very careful before dismissing the great myths as just childish stories from the childhood of the world. They warned us to be careful about dismissing our dreams as just so much nonsense. We are still trying to discover what they meant.

. . . whoever does not receive the kingdom of God like a child shall not enter it. Mark 10:15

A Changing Face

People constantly come and go, passing in and out of focus in front of our human lens. A cartoon in *The New Yorker* illustrates what I mean. It was a strip cartoon, about five or six sections to it. A man points a polaroid camera at nothing, he clicks it, and as he stands there, gradually about twelve feet away, a person appears. At first the outline is vague, then it becomes more definite, and finally it is solid.

The moment I saw that cartoon I thought of someone, a person I have lately became aware of as changing. I don't know why or how, but they quite certainly are changing. A few years ago they looked almost invisible. They were quiet, chronically quiet. They were shy to a painful extent. There was a tendency to be overweight, to be withdrawn, to be totally lacking in any self-confidence or self-assertion.

Suddenly they have begun to change. The texture of the face is different. It is less drawn, more mobile. The eyes are showing interest, movements are easier and more graceful. Body language, as we say these days, is beginning to cry out that the person is alive, is a person, has things to say and do.

It is more than an illusion of mine. Other people have noticed it. But the point I want to make is the necessity for each one of us to be aware of the infinite possibilities for change which lie in any human being at any time. It is so easy to consign an acquaintance, an employee, a client to a certain category. That is not necessarily wrong as long as we are open to the fact that, precisely because they are a human being, they are full of possibilities. That same humanity has infinite capacity to unsettle our neat categorizing, to refuse to conform to our presuming portraiture. The reason is, of course, that within that humanity there is a greater image reflected, a glory hidden, a divinity poised for ever new creativity.

. . . until we all attain . . . to mature humanity, to the measure of the stature of the fulness of Christ. Ephesians 4:13

Four Horsemen

I was flicking through a *New Yorker*, and suddenly there they were. There were four figures on motorbikes, all of them figures to inspire fear and loathing. On one huge bike was the familiar skeleton under a great cloak, its bony hands grasping the handlebars. On another sat a great armoured form, its face hidden by a plumed helmet. Each of the four was different, and all were spectres of terror.

It is strange how powerful an effect certain images have. Nearly twenty-four centuries ago, at a time of anxiety and dread in the history of Israel, one of their great prophets conjured up an image to describe how people were feeling about the world of their time. He described the coming of four great horsemen riding across the world. That image lived vividly and dreadfully. It was given a name, "The Four Horsemen of the Apocalypse."

Centuries went by, and there emerged from Israel another movement, which came to be called Christianity. Near the end of the first century of the Christian era, a writer named John of Patmos wrote his visions, his Revelation as he called it. It was about the turbulent and anxious era he and others were living through. As imagery for his own time he used "The Four Horsemen of the Apocalypse," the great shadowed images of war, plague, famine, death.

Again in the fourteenth century they appear as an image of that terrible era of plague. Is it not interesting to see them the subject of a whimsical cartoon in the pages of a witty sophisticated twentieth century magazine, to see them again as the name of a movie dealing with the obscenity and meaninglessness of this century's most terrible war — all as if voicing our suspicion that, though things change on the surface, they remain the same underneath. We are still aware at the deepest level of our being of the enemies that stalk the shadowed places of our humanity.

. . . the great day of their wrath has come, and who can stand before it? Revelation 6:17

Morality

Without being able to be precise about it, one can feel in the air a kind of wheel of human behaviour and attitudes coming full cycle.

Generally speaking, within the lifetime of most middle-aged adults, western society operated in a certain way. By and large it was understood that there were certain elements of consensus about personal and social morality. From a point sometime after the Second World War, for an immense and interconnected number of reasons, that general consensus about how life was to be lived was shattered.

I wish merely to attempt to express one huge change. In western society, somewhere between 1945 and now, maybe somewhere in those tempestuous 1960s, the individual became more important than the community. I cringe at the unavoidable oversimplification of that, but I think it stands as a generalization.

We now look at a very popular magazine *Psychology Today*, and we hear a very much listened to American sociologist, Daniel Yankelovich, saying that today's adult generation, who moved from the older world of moral consensus to a multi-choice or, to use another word, *permissive* atmosphere of the last two decades, are now alarmed at the total lack, or seeming total lack, of moral criteria for a new generation. A parental generation, who had at least some remembered moral criteria on which to base judgements about the many choices of a multi-lifestyle world, are now realizing that the more the future becomes multi-choice, the more, rather than less, do we need moral criteria.

I smile when I read these things because, if those spoil-sport religious people talked like this, they would be dismissed as sermonizing.

The law of the Lord is perfect, reviving the soul; The precepts of the Lord are right. Psalm 19: 7,8

Hospital

Madonna

In the last few years both the interior and exterior of the nearby hospital have changed very much. Quite often I find myself in those corridors. There are the things you see in every hospital. The floors shimmer, the odd mysterious trolley rolls by with this or that piece of technology, the dull overall murmer of visitors' voices vibrates through the hall.

A group of people are waiting to be admitted. There are the non-commital questions, the clicking of typewriters, the crisp uniforms, the volunteers moving around with magazines and candies. There at the centre is the information desk, where a hundred human lives flick round and round in alphabetical order in a circular file, their cards, as they must be, neatly catalogued. Within that flickering file are faces; in those cards are pain and dread and loneliness mingled with hope and joy and recovery. In those cards are eyes and voices and parched lips and hands reaching out.

But over the door there is a particularly powerful symbol. It is very simple. A nurse is holding a child to her shoulder. She is not glamourized; she is real. The attitude is not sentimental, not extravagant. It is quiet, unaffected, natural. In fact, this photograph is a modern madonna. It provides something very difficult to find in our infinitely plural culture, a symbol that communicates a universal message instantly, without at the same time being trite. It speaks of something eternal, beyond all the pulsations and murmurings of human life. It speaks of acceptance, compassion, humanity.

. . thou didst form my inward parts, thou didst knit me together in my mother's womb. I praise thee! Psalm 139: 13,14

A Loving Hand

I never cease to marvel at the associations fashioned by our minds. I am in the outpatients clinic in this city hospital. I am standing near two people who are having a conversation. One is a doctor, fairly young, the other is a man, elderly and rather frail. The older man has been brought to hospital because he has not been feeling very well, and there has been a bit of worrying medical history The doctor is chatting to him. He is trying to get as much background information as he can. From his attitude it is very obvious that he is a very caring person. In the course of the conversation, someone else in the clinic comes up to the doctor and says something about another patient. The doctor, because he does not want to interrupt the old man, takes a pen from his pocket and writes the name of the other person on the skin of the back of his hand. A simple thing, but for me it sent a kind of sonar echo across twenty-seven centuries.

It was a grim time for a nation. They had seen their country ravished, and thousands had been taken into exile. It was an invitation to hopelessness and cynicism. Yet a great poet — his name was Isaiah — wrote an unforgetable line in which he forged the image of the love of a God who was the eternal lover in every circumstance.

"Behold," Isaiah has God say to his people, "I have graven thee upon the palms of my hands."

I though of that twenty-seven hundred year old image of the love of God as I saw a doctor write a patient's name on the back of his hand, because he wished to remember and to respond.

Behold, I have graven you on the palms of my hands . . .
Isaiah 49:16

The Face of Love

Supper time in the hospital; the corridors are relatively quiet. It is that hour between the comings and goings of visitors. The staff seems to be under less pressure; everybody's movements are less tense. Along the wide and cheerfully lit corridors some people are sitting in chairs. There are three or four elderly individuals, eating slowly and deliberately, gazing at the opposite wall, thinking their own thoughts.

A little further down I saw the couple. They too were elderly. She was in a wheelchair; he was sitting on a chair facing her. Obviously he had come for a visit. He had taken off his jacket because he had all the time in the world for this visit. It wasn't a task taken from more important things in his life. It *was* his life.

She was very weak, and he had come to help with supper. Lovingly and gently he was helping her to eat. To avoid seeming to be feeding a child, he was quietly chatting away in Chinese, letting her hear the familiar voice of many years, that familiarity which often pierces our dim senses when nothing else will.

Later, when I came back along the corridor, they were still there. By this time he had produced a little jar of some food he had brought from home, and they were sharing it. They could have been in their own home, so oblivious were they and so unselfconscious. Probably in her own mind she was at home. However, I shall never know that. I know only that, as I walked down the stairs of the hospital, I reflected on those words of St Paul which I quote on this page. He wrote them twenty centuries ago, but they will live until the world ends.

Charity beareth all things. Charity never faileth.
1 Corinthians 13:7,8

Ethel

When you are continually involved in the lives of people, you come to notice a great deal. I thought of that as we walked away from the hospital a few weeks ago and we spoke about her. We had just left her, having seen that she was as comfortable as possible in her unavoidable restlessness.

A small thing had struck me that evening when I arrived in the room. You know there is a room in life, perhaps more than any other room, where there is no space for anything else but honesty, where no personality masks are worn. In that sense it is a kind of confessional. It's the space created in a hospital ward when the beige curtain is swung around the bed and we act out, in that little theatre, whatever scene of our human drama we are involved in.

She was there, fragile, restless, a little distraught. Quite clear at times, elusive at other moments. And it was her hair I noticed. It was long and gathered up from her head in a kind of crown, and in the middle there was a large comb. I'm groping for words. It was a style I associate with many decades ago, a style seen in oval frames and long ago brown coloured photographs. And she didn't want it brushed or combed. She was vehement about that. And I suddenly remembered.

I remembered her coming to me a few months previously, probably when she felt unwell at first, and showing me a photograph of herself and her sister as young women in a long ago English garden. And she showed it to me in a way that was really saying, "You see me old and bent and white haired, but look and see who I really am." And from that long-ago moment there looked a dark haired girl, her hair swept up and gathered in what was the height of fun and fashion. And I realized that, although I was in a hospital ward, she was far away in an English garden.

. . . *now we see in a mirror dimly, but then face to face.*
1 Corinthians 13:12

Prayer and Therapy

In a hospital room I was bending over a friend who had already withdrawn from contact and was stepping out on the great journey from this life. I had chosen to say very quietly the twenty-third psalm, "The Lord is my shepherd," and after a few moments I heard him join me in those words across a widening gulf between our worlds.

Coming away that evening, I found myself thinking that so much would be given to all of us if only we would not make water-tight compartments into which we put various human experiences. Consider words such as *prayer* and *therapy*. Many of us would put the first in a file called "religion" and the second in a file called "medicine" or maybe "psychology." We would not of course be wrong, but neither would we be right. The sad thing is that we have nearly lost the capacity to understand religious words and concepts and symbols as therapeutic or, to use a simpler and more inclusive word, as healing.

As a society in general, we see religion as being about ideas, concepts, institutions, rules, inhibitions, dogmas. There are many reasons for this and, yes, the blame lies partly on the church; but there are all sorts of other factors that have brought it about.

The sad thing is that waiting in the wings of human consciousness is the great and lovely language that has long been part of the Judaeo-Christian heritage. Here are words like forgiveness, freedom, resurrection, reconciliation, hope, faith, love, joy, peace, shalom. The list could go on much longer. All those words are used by a thousand transient therapies of our time, some of them costly and some even manipulative. Yet those words are the ancient treasures of church and synagogue which we are in danger of forgetting.

Heaven and earth will pass away, but my words will not pass away. Luke 21:33

Words of Power

It is that time of night when the hospital corridors are empty and the building has the quietness it develops when most visitors are gone. There is a kind of settling down for the night. Given the realities of hospitals, that settling down is never absolute, but the atmosphere does change and become muted.

Someone was dying and for quite a while — over a number of weeks — there had been opportunities to talk. But now the time had come when he was beginning to turn away and to orient himself for the great journey that had to be taken. It is the time when, as it seems to me sometimes, even our deepest and longest loves begin to be exchanged for a greater and more mysterious love which awaits us.

So it was with my friend. He had turned outward for the great journey and was no longer responding. As he lay peacefully, I did what priests before me have done for thousands of years. Quietly, while I bent over his head on the pillow, I repeated words and images of infinite beauty and power which he had known all his life. And he who had already begun to leave, who had moved beyond even naming those with whom he had shared life to the uttermost, was called by those ancient images. His voice joined mine, and together we said, "The Lord is my shepherd, therefore can I lack nothing. He shall lead me beside still waters. He shall restore my soul. Yea, though I walk through the valley of the shadow of death, I will fear no evil." For him those words possessed great power. Their very sound, the images they conveyed, were therapeutic.

In such moments we stumble on the mysterious power of language. No wonder the apostle John says that the Word was God.

. . . *speak the word only, and my servant shall be healed.*
Matthew 8:8

Listening

For the last hour or so I have been admitted to somebody's life. Not of course to all of it, but to aspects, troubled parts, questions, unresolved things — material that simply has to be shared. To do this is always a privilege. It is something that another human being gives to one. It is a trust not lightly dealt with. But what has struck me again is how little I said, or indeed needed to say, in that period.

I listened. But listening is not effortless, not if you have really decided to give the other person the gift of your listening, in return for their giving you the gift of their spoken trust. But as often as one experiences this unspoken contract, one is intrigued by the therapy one both receives and gives in listening.

I have a dream. One day our society will create an order, a profession if you will. The members of this order will be selected by all of us, emerging from us by some natural process. There will be no colleges to train them. They will not be subsidized by the government, because then they would have fifty forms to fill out each day and they would, like the rest of us, go slowly mad. They will be called simply "listeners." There will be no advancement in their work. They will be able to leave it when they wish. They may be any age as long as ear and mind are clear. They need to speak no particular language except the universal tongue of understanding and compassion.

A dream? Perhaps. Or perhaps it will be so on another planet and in another time. Perhaps it will be so in what men and women of faith call the kingdom.

Bear one another's burdens, and so fulfil the law of Christ.
Galations 6:2

Sainthood

How is one to describe another human being? How is one to express all the complexity and subtlety that another life contains? Above all, how does one articulate the beauty of humanity when one encounters it?

Let me use other words. How do you talk about sainthood? I don't mean stained glass window sainthood but the flesh and blood kind, the kind heard in a voice, felt in a touch, seen shining from a pair of eyes. It is a sainthood that does not judge but affirms, that is rich not merely in goodness but in humour, not merely in holiness but in laughter. Above all it is totally natural and honest.

To get some exercise, I avoid the elevator and walk up the stairs of the hospital. I turn, walk along the corridor, and find the room. I am greeted by a smile that I know has had to emerge from considerable discomfort. I hear welcoming and good-humoured words that I know have had to be found in the face of understandable worry and fear. There is some chit-chat about the situation, about what is being done, what the doctor is saying, what may be ahead in the next few days. Then we are chatting about others. I find myself being asked how I myself am. Eventually we link hands for a moment and commend ourselves to God.

As I leave, I keep on thinking of the wonder of some human beings. In this half-hour I have been as much visited as this person of whom I speak. In a deep sense they have visited me. They have become grace to me. By being beside that bed, I have become the richer. I have at some level been healed.

Blessed are they whose strength is in thee, in whose heart are the highways to Zion. Psalm 84:5

Faith

The trouble with that old *Reader's Digest* phrase, "the most unforgettable character I've ever met," is that one meets that character so often! What I mean is that, if one is sensitive and open to the possibilities in human lives, one is constantly coming across unforgettable aspects of people, discovering pieces of them that they reveal whether or not they mean to.

I would introduce someone by name, but that of course I cannot do. But meet her now because she is worth meeting. She is elderly yet more alive and adventurous than some people thirty years younger. In earlier years she lived in the northland in places from which most of us would run away in terror. Most of the time she did what she had to do for very basic payment. Tomorrow she faces surgery. We chat about that. You realize as you listen to her that she has no fear at all. What's more, you realize that lack of fear is in her voice and in her eyes. Those are the places that tell the truth over and above the words any of us use to cover fear.

Why this total lack of fear? Is it lack of imagination? A lack of sensitivity? Not caring about life any more? It is none of these things. She possesses a gift that some of us would totally dismiss as an unreality. Maybe the occasional very sad person might sneer at it. Some with insight and maturity would recognize it as perhaps the most precious possession a human being can have. She possesses total faith and trust in the love and providence of God. Because of that, when you have been with her, she has strengthened you rather than you her.

You emerge from visiting her realizing that you have been visited, and you feel very grateful.

Jesus said, O woman, great is thy faith. Matthew 15:28

Release

We were chatting in the late evening. The particular part of the hospital was rather cut off from the rest. It seemed to be almost a little world in itself. Supper was long over, and the various activities of the psychiatric ward were going on. Here and there a group chatted. Over here a few people watched television. Near the door someone was chatting on the phone. One or two restless people wandered hither and yon.

We looked around to find a corner where one could chat. It wasn't easy. We found a couple of chairs, tried to blot out the sounds of the TV, and began.

At times our conversation took off, and sometimes it floundered. After all, someone had been through a great deal. There had been an operation, a lot of pain, a lot of feeling that life was really over. Even though much love had come to give support, there was still a feeling of great struggle. Now there was an onslaught of deep depression which had to be battled.

We talked mainly about loved ones. We chatted about possibilities ahead, after this difficult chapter. There were long gaps, difficult silences. Then suddenly I was being told of some conversations earlier that day, sessions with a psychiatrist. The voice became a little more alive. I asked how things had gone in the session, when there would be another one. And soon I learned what had been felt in those sessions, how anger at certain things had swept over him and he had begun to express it and it had felt very good. I looked and saw the dead eyes coming alive and the lips beginning to smile. It was so good to see someone being released from an inner prison.

. . .*you will know the truth and the truth will make you free.* John 8:32

All Good Gifts

I had not been able to park in the lot; so I looked around and there happened to be a space in front of the hospital. I was glad because it was raining hard. I had already been wet a few times that day, and I didn't relish the idea of being wet again. Head down, shoulders huddled in the way we all do, I headed for the emergency entrance, which happened to be the nearest.

In this particular hospital the emergency entrance is right beside the exit where patients are discharged. Just as I was going inside, a couple came out. I would say they were in their forties. She looked drawn and rather pale, as if she had been through a fairly long siege.

What struck me was the way she betrayed intense happiness in every nuance of her being — voice, face, eyes. She was brought to the entrance in the usual wheelchair, and at that precise moment I arrived. Somebody was holding an umbrella for her, yet what she obviously wanted to do was to register, by every means she could, that she was outside, that she was free! A little gingerly she stepped out of the wheelchair. Then, before getting into the car, she deliberately put her face up to the sky and let some raindrops fall on her face. She said something. I didn't catch it because it was cried out ecstatically, an expression of great joy and life and freedom.

The door closed and the car turned out toward the street. I stood there and felt the rain on my head and on my shoulders, and I understood something in a new way. I lifted my face for a moment to the grey sky and realized that to be free to feel the touch of creation is a gift beyond price.

> *For the beauty of the earth,*
> *For the glory of the skies,*
> *Lord of all, to thee we raise,*
> *This our sacrifice of praise.*

F.S. Pierpoint

Sacred Heart

A moment's carelessness on a wet lakeside dock, a tumble, and sud
denly there was a broken wrist. After X-rays it turned out that i
would need a general anaesthetic; so I had to do all the things tha
line one up for the operating room.

It was a very busy day in surgery, especially for orthopedics; sc
evening wore on before the stretcher came and one slid clumsily on
to the narrow surface, to begin that peculiarly passive journey that
most of us at some time or other have taken. One watches the ceiling go by, blinking under the white lights, bumping slightly now
and then, sometimes seeing faces float past, entering the elevator
and finally the very different atmosphere of the surgery area.

I want to mention only a particular few minutes that had
significance for me. They arose from something quite fortuitous.
Thinking that the surgeon was ready for us, the nurse did this and
that and wheeled me into the theatre. She then placed little patches
that connected my body with the electrocardiogram, then she left.

Eventually it turned out that the surgeon was delayed in an
emergency. That fifteen to twenty minutes of silence and stillness
and solitude became very profound. I tried to give myself to it, to
receive it as a gift. First there was only the thin high tone of my own
heartbeat registering on the machine somewhere behind me.
Gradually I began to notice the slight noises of the operating room
equipment. Beyond them I became aware of the life of the hospital
itself, beating and stirring and murmuring like a great heart, full of
joy and anxiety, sleep and restlessness, pain, loving care, humanity. As the moments of seeming silence passed by, they became
deeper and deeper, richer and richer, until I recalled a symbol common in the Ireland of my childhood, the sacred heart of Jesus
beating eternally at the centre of the universe.

. . . *one God and Father of us all, who is above all and through all
and in all.* Ephesians 4:6

Downtown

Macbeth

I am watching one of the worlds great tragedies. In front of me on the stage, which at once is remarkably bare yet enables my imagination to fill it with what I wish, sits a king who is not a king. I am watching Macbeth at Stratford. I watch him sit alone on his crude throne and nervously put his hands to the unfamiliar crown he wears. I watch him come to terms with a new realization that is at once very old in the long story of the human quest for power. "To be thus," he says, "is nothing. To be safely thus is everything."

One realizes that Macbeth is coming to the chilling realization of the terrible lie which is at the heart of our quest for power. Power promises but does not produce what we really long for. It deludes us that we wish it when our real longing is for another, and the name of our real longing is security. Power whispers to Macbeth that if Duncan is murdered Macbeth will taste power. But the next whisper is that Banquo must be killed to feel secure. Then it needs Fleance (Banquo's son) to be killed. One more step is always needed to capture the elusive shadow called security.

We need to realize that nations are no different. We possess vast powers as a civilization but we always feel the need of one more, just one more weapon system, for the gaining at last of security. Maybe on both sides of the world we should deliberately name the next family of super weapons Macbeth, Duncan, Banquo, Fleance. As we impoverish our budgets and wrestle with our national and international souls, the names would at least remind us of the subtle deceits of power and security.

. . . *whosoever will be chief among you, let him be your servant:* . . . Matthew 20:27

Ghandhi

I had occasion to go again to see the movie *Ghandhi*. I suspect that its success is due to something even deeper than the portrait of goodness and greatness it gives. I realized this time, as I had not before, that the real greatness of the film may well be in the honour it does to the political.

What does one mean by that? I thought of this as I read again the other day a timeless statement made by one to whom Ghandhi frequently referred — Jesus of Nazareth. On one occasion Jesus said, "Render to Caesar the things that are Caesar's, and to God the things that are God's." But that response has always created an agonized counter question. What is Caesar's and what is God's?

In the long ago Indian situation, and I think with integrity in the movie, there is a counterpoint between Ghandhi and the group of friends who form about him. He, Ghandhi, possesses a vision of the absolute — absolute love, absolute brotherhood, absolute mutual acceptance of Hindu and Moslem. For this he is ready to do absolute actions including offering his life. About him are men, I think, essentially of no less human quality, who see that the absolute cannot be given embodiment within history. What has to be sought in history, and human affairs, whether we like to admit it or not, is the acceptable political reality.

One of the tragedies of public existence in our society is the inescapably pejoritive quality we have given to the word *political*. In its acceptance of the necessity of the political reality; the film *Ghandhi* does honour to a much beleaguered political process.

Let us now praise famous men.
Ecclesiasticus 44:1

Monstrance

Years ago Bram Stoker, perhaps without realizing it, set a fashion in linking horror and religion. It has now become almost a cliché in the canon of popular horror that vampires are sent reeling by the sudden appearance of a crucifix. In fact, in recent years we witnessed a supreme comment on the late twentieth century being so very different from the late nineteenth. When, in the latest remake of Dracula (starring Frank Langelli), the crucifix is produced in a confrontation with Dracula, instead of recoiling, the vampire dismisses the gesture with impatient contempt.

All that came to my mind because the other day I was relearning something I had forgotten, that the words *monstrance* and *monster* and *demonstration* are all from the same root. First, what is a monstrance? It is the vessel or instrument that traditionally has been used to show publically the sacred wafer or host in the Mass or Eucharist. To show the host was to demonstrate a great mystery or, to use another word, to help men and women experience a sense of the numinous, the presence of the mysterious, the spiritual, the divine.

This makes one think. Why are we in an era of endless horror movies and horror stories? Because there is abroad in the air of our time a deep sense of the mystery and terror of human existence. I suspect that beyond the horror stories, the blood drenched movies, is hiding somewhere one of the most religious generations this planet has ever seen. Between the monstrance displaying the sacred host of sacramental worship and the monster shambling and gibbering on the screen, there is a very thin dividing line.

. . . you have not received the spirit of bondage again to fear; but you have received the Spirit of adoption, whereby we cry, Abba, Father. Romans 8:15

The Pyx

It was an article about the return of the horror movie in the 1980s. These days it is of course a new kind of horror. The monster no longer shambles around in the dark night outside the heroine's cottage, the monster is no longer wholesomely hideous and healthily tangible. Today the monster is usually satanic and intangible. It doesn't attack anybody and run off into the woods. It occupies people, making their eyes shimmer and their voices change. One movie title in particular rang a bell. It was called *The Pyx*. Religion is popular in today's horror movies, but it is religion with a twist. It is never religion in the sense of joy and celebration and love, but religion in the sense of the mysterious, the awesome, the occult. It really made me smile, and when I take you with me to the reality of *The Pyx* you will know why.

In the cathedral it is kept near one of the altars in a tiny compartment. I go there, open the door, take it out, put it around my neck, and go out. I get into the car and head for a home or hospital, as I did a few days ago. There in a ward we met. She was elderly and frail and full of courage and hope. We chatted for a while. Then we did what she has done so often at the cathedral altar. We shared the bread of the Eucharist.

It wasn't long after the operation, and she really was not ready for a long recitation of words. So on that bedside table lay the pyx, a small silver box that carried bread consecrated at the Eucharist in the cathedral and reserved for such as her. When the simple timeless act of communion was over we said "goodbye." She was happy because she was part of a family in the eating of that bread. The pyx had carried the bread of her joy.

You see, there was nothing occult, nothing fearsome, nothing exotic. In spite of the movie industry God is one who approaches us and touches us in the ordinary, the everyday, the human.

. . . God did not give us a spirit of timidity but a spirit of power and love and self control. 2 Timothy 1:7

The Music of God

I wonder who it is who writes the program notes for the concerts of our symphony orchestra. He or she writes from the safe stronghold of anonymity. But I would like to quote a gem that reveals a whole set of assumptions in that unknown mind.

The commentator is writing about the French composer Poulenc who has composed some of the world's finest organ music. At some stage in the remarks the commentator says, "He was known during his lifetime as a man of urbanity and wit, qualities that appeared conspicuously in his music even when, late in life, he turned with increasing frequency to religious subjects."

Dear me, what a tragedy is implied! There is the gifted and creative Poulenc — urbane, witty, pouring out this beautiful music, a brilliant conversationalist, the soul of wit, the life of the party, probably on everybody's invitation list — and, by jove, if the fellow doesn't go and get religion! Naturally it follows as night follows day that that will be the end of all we like best about Poulenc. No longer will there be brilliant remarks, no more witty exchanges, no urbane reflections. His music will get stodgy and heavy and religious and mediocre; and God knows what, if you will pardon us, will happen to the fine musician.

But to everybody's surprise this does not happen. Poulenc does not get stodgy and heavy and mediocre. He sparkles. He becomes even wittier. He is more, not less, urbane. His music has all it had before, and amazingly it seems to have even more. Good heavens, is it possible to be all that and religious too!

I feel that I want to say to our local writer of notes for our symphony concerts, "Believe it or not, it is." Check with Sydney Smith, Malcolm Muggeridge, St Francis of Assisi, and a host of other Christians, and you will find that it is not so extraordinary that faith and joy mix with the most interesting consequences.

Thou dost show me the path of life; in thy presence there is fullness of joy, in thy right hand are pleasures for evermore.
Psalm 16:11

Changing History

I found myself pulled up short by witnessing the moment. It was at a meeting of a group who were deciding the musical pieces that each of them would sing at a recital that was being planned. The suggestion was made of a particularly lovely song cycle by Schumann entitled *Frauen Liebe und Leben* (Woman's Love and Life). As you would expect, it is a cycle extolling the loveliness and worth of that aspect of a woman's life. But when the possibility of singing it was offered to one person, the reply was, "No, I don't wish to sing that because it's sexist."

Now let's begin by saying that anybody who wishes to do so has a perfect right to say that anything is sexist should they think it is. But until I heard that particular statement about that particular piece of music, I had not realized that the charge of sexism was becoming a device by which we deny the past.

I recall some years ago that it used to be fashionable to dredge up examples of how Soviet ideology dictated that writers and historians should deny the reality of the past and redesign it to become more suitable to a contempory ideology. I felt that Schumann's song cycle was a lovely nineteenth century expression of art and life rendered in terms that were then seen and understood and lived. To deny those understandings in the context of their own time is pointless and sad. To refuse to sing the cycle because now in a different context it may seem sexist, is to deny the rich long process of the developing human story. In endorsing the present sensitivity about sexist language, sexist gestures, and assumptions, we do not have to deny history.

. . . all these though well attested by their faith, did not receive what was promised, since God had foreseen something better for us. . . .Hebrews 11:39

Success

Somebody phoned to talk about a person whom they love very much. They were very worried about him. In all that they said, one phrase stood out. "He feels deeply," the concerned voice said to me, "that he is a failure at 50."

The conversation continued. That phrase made me realize the peculiar limitation in the ways in which we judge success and failure. I happened to know the person in question, and to me as an observer there was certainly no question of failure. True, in the job that he does extremely well, he had not moved into the higher levels. But from where I stood, one could see a number of things very clearly. One could see a man doing a job in a way that had earned him the gratitude of at least hundreds of people, that made him be regarded as utterly dependable and deeply respected. One could see a man who had been capable of a rich relationship with an attractive woman for almost a quarter of a century, who had formed and guided three children through the chasms of recent decades and helped them to become fine young adults in a very difficult world. Yet not one of these criteria is used by our society in judging this hollow tyrant we call success. The one criteria for that is the seductive mistress we call career, profession, job.

About a week later I looked at him over a restaurant table and saw his eyes fill as I tried to list the categories of his real success, the things I have mentioned in these few lines. I suspect that you know why they affected him. They affected him because nobody ever before had put them into spoken words.

There are so many terribly important things we never think of saying because we think they are too simple or too obvious. Let them be but spoken, and they are richly healing and creative.

Lord, . . . only say the word and my servant will be healed.
Matthew 8:8

Lost Treasure

A small incident, it was no more than a snatch of conversation heard across a city restaurant. It's a spot in which you see a fair number of older people. They come for a morning coffee or an afternoon cup of tea. Most of the time I notice that they are alone.

An elderly person is sitting alone. She has just finished a snack and is fixing up the small bill. She hands the money and the bill to the waitress who is a young girl. Then, because the old lady wishes to make some friendly proposition, she murmurs to the young girl, "The widow's mite," and she smiles. She presumes that her allusion will be understood. It isn't. The waitress, who is a pleasant and helpful girl, is puzzled. She makes some questioning sound. The older woman repeats her phrase again. The young girl is still totally mystified, and they part with an uncomprehending smile from the waitress and a sad slightly embarrassed look on the older face.

I realize that I have been witness to an example of a great culture gap between two generations. I am not particularly claiming higher culture for one but merely pointing to a great difference. The older woman is a member of the last generation in western society whose imagery, language, and thought forms are almost unconsciously formed by a treasury of great literature. Most of this treasury the younger woman has lost. The book I refer to in this case, of course, is the English Bible.

Perhaps the even greater tragedy is that the younger woman doesn't realize what she has lost. That still holds true even if you are considering the Bible not as a repository of faith but only as great literature.

Thy testimonies are my heritage for ever; yea, they are the joy of my heart. Psalm 119:111

The Timeless Gods

As always there is, in the neighbouring block, a new restaurant. What shall I say this eating place seeks to be? Attractive, gentle, feminine without being effeminate. It aims for that gentle world which many restaurants are aiming for nowadays. There is a faint air of nostalgia in the decor. There is gentle music played on what sounds like a phonograph of bygone days. For all I know, they manufacture every element of this atmosphere today in some computerized factory in California. There are lots of potted plants and light fragile chairs and some flowers and a little wrought iron here and there.

It is all determinedly contemporary in the paradoxically nostalgic way that we are seeking the chic and the contemporary today. Today the way to create the ultimate in contemporary environment is to simulate any other era. That too must surely be telling us something about the times, but to even mention that is to digress.

It was something else that caught one'e attention. Over at one end there was a line of plants. Behind them was a lamp, dim and intimate. Above the corner shone a lamp in a dark blue shade. I began to notice that from time to time a young person would get up from a table, disappear behind the plants, and after a while return. Then I realized that with afternoon tea you could indulge yourself in something that has fascinated people for centuries. You could get your teacup read.

So one by one these young sophisticates in the heart of a modern city showed how timeless the ancient gods really are. We haven't left them behind in Delphi and Babylon and Olympus and Thebes! The sacred grove is there in the city for the entering. Here sits a twittering matronly oracle willing to read your life and love in a teacup, crumpets and jam on the side.

. . . do not be anxious about tomorrow, for tomorrow will be anxious for itself. Matthew 6:34

Lounge Bar

Because a great deal of my working life is spent downtown, I sometimes find myself there at a very late hour. This evening it is clear and cold; the well-lit canyon of towers is glittering and scrubbed against the night sky.

I have cause to walk with someone across to the underground parking lot at one of the hotels. Those raw and cavernous basements, lurking beneath the plush foyers and offices, can be the outer edges of the jungle that merges with the thin veneer of urban civilization.

As I return, having seen someone to a car, I come back through the ground floor of the hotel. The foyer is almost deserted. the night staff leisurely moving this way and that. From the lounge bar there float out the soft easy meandering notes of the piano. It echoes as if alone, sounding in a room where empty chairs and tables have done with the day. I look in to where the pianist is gazing into some weary distance far beyond the mirrored walls, his hands moving as if apart from him. Two people are still seated at a table, a thin column of cigarette smoke gropes upward for the ceiling. One figure is at the bar counter, his body leaning in the timeless posture of one tired of the day but unable to welcome sleep.

There is about it all an air of svelte melancholy. Here, in this little universe of lined up glasses and wicker chairs, the world ends not with a bang, but with a tinkling whimper.

Those that look through the windows are dimmed and the doors on the street are shut;. . . and all the daughters of song are brought low . . .Ecclesiastes 12:3,4

The Magic Walking Stick

The dreams of childhood die very hard. I presume it's because at that stage everything is new, everything is unexpected, and above all we have not decided, or had decided for us, what is impossible; so therefore everything is possible.

The other day I was in a drug store which is at the entrance of a medical-dental building near the cathedral. On the way out I saw a stand in which they had for sale about a dozen walking sticks. There were various types with various handles. Suddenly my mind placed me in front of a certain page in a long-ago book. Without any difficulty I went back into the book and into the long-forgotten world where it once took me.

It seemed, so the story went, to be a totally ordinary walking stick found by a totally ordinary boy. But of course it was not ordinary at all. It had the most wonderful properties. Accidently one day the boy found that, if he twisted the walking stick in his hand and thought of a far-away country, he would suddenly find himself whirled through some mysterious reality, and there he would be. I have now long forgotten the details of the various destinations. There was among them, I know, an endless golden beach backed by impenetrable jungle.

Alas, the boy lost the stick. Ever afterwards he would look for it. In houses, shops, coatracks, he went on looking for the magic walking stick for a long time. He never found it, but the book also said that any boy who had read the book should, just in case, keep an eye out for it. I confess I did that for a long time. The other day in the drug store, forty years later, I ran my eyes over the walking sticks they had for sale. I wasn't really expecting, you understand, but I looked just in case. Anyway, the day one finally ceases to look for a magic walking stick, that is the day to give up.

People who speak thus make it clear that they are seeking a homeland. Hebrews 11:14

The Prie-Dieu

The antique shop was a large one. I found myself in it only because the family was in a nearby store, and since I am not a shopper by nature, I was just putting in time.

Near the back and standing half hidden among elderly pieces of furniture, I saw it. It was obviously among those pieces that were not expected to raise a great price, and therefore it was not presented very attractively. It was dusty and rather battered. It was what you once called a prie-dieu, a simple padded wooden kneeler with a front rail on which to lean as you knelt. Prie-dieu simply means "before God." That simple piece of furniture would have come either from a small church or a chapel or perhaps a confessional booth. Its placement in the antique store seemed to symbolize a sad and contradictory thing. Many people in our society would view all that the old confessional prie-dieu stands for as passé. Who needs, they might well say, a system where we kneel in childish dependence to whisper the self-doubts and guilts and fears of our humanity to a far away and debatable god? After all, we are mature modern people!

The ironic thing, however, is that in our society millions of people hunger for a relationship in which they can share those same timeless self-doubts and fears and guilts. Sometimes we turn to the army of professional listeners we have recruited — counsellors, psychologists, psychiatrists. We carry out in their offices what countless people did on this old prayer kneeler. They called it confessing their sins. However, we feel such language to be moralistic and judgmental. We have other language. In the sixties we called it " letting it all hang out." In the eighties it's "telling your story." But the fact of the matter is that it is, and always will be, our confession.

Jesus told them a parable to the effect that they ought always to pray and not lose heart. Luke 18:1

Earthrise

I was in a photographer's picking up a picture which needed to be framed again. While I was waiting, I looked around at some equipment. I picked up one piece of a camera, noticed it was a Hasselblad, and remarked that Hasselblad must be the Mercedes Benz of the camera world, and just about as expensive. It seems to be so often the professional's camera.

There and then I learned from someone about a place where you and I could have a magnificent Hasselblad absolutely free, if only we could get to it. As a matter of fact, if we could get there we could pick up no less than twelve of them absolutely free.

They all lie in the dust of the moon, scattered with the other debris that the last moon probe jettisoned to make room, and to lose weight, for the moon rocks that the astronauts wished to bring home. Twelve Hasselblads in perfect working condition lie scattered in that faraway silent place.

The thought I particularly wanted to share is the lovely prize that one of those cameras gave us before we left it there. At some moment in the hours of that transient human visit to the moon, a man held one of those Hasselblad, pointed its viewfinder at the distant jagged ridge that bounded his horizon, and waited. Slowly, and with infinite loveliness and majesty, there rose above that ridge a huge ball. It hung there shimmering and flashing with a score of colours. The contrast with the deadness of the moon was total. The lovely ball was glittering like a diamond, blue and white, brown and green.

The astronaut pressed the shutter. Of all the photographs taken in this century, that one was to change our whole concept of life. Its effect is still spreading. It is generally called Earthrise. You probably have seen it very frequently. It is really a great modern ikon.

The earth is the Lord's and the fullness thereof, the world, and those who dwell therein. . . . Psalm 24:1

The Computer Store

It was situated in a long line of undistinguished store fronts. I had made a promise that we would go and look at home computers. We had set out, the two of us from the family, my son at fourteen intensely interested in computers, myself dutifully in attendance. However, while I may be technologically ignorant, my aging senses are very much on the alert as we go in.

The store immediately communicates, or shall I say it works hard at creating, a future environment. The various pieces of hardware sit gleaming on their bases, their screens flashing, their buttons gleaming. Racks of brightly coloured magazines shout their specialized language. Under glass are smaller pieces of equipment. On the wall are posters rich in words like *tomorrow, future, breakthrough*. Over on another wall the dour face of Mr Spock from *Startrek* gazes out at me from the imaginary television world of the twenty-third century.

Yet one has only to look beyond the well-placed spotlights to see the old framework of the store. As we stand around pressing buttons and looking at tomorrow, the lights flicker and the owner wonders out loud about the possibility of a power failure.

I cannot help but see a parable, a symbol. The future is always struggling to be born inside the present. We humans have an extraordinary capacity to dream our way out of the limited present to the next step of the future. This sad little building is itself not even of today; it is of yesterday. Yet it is this ordinary corner of the city to which my child comes to find the magic doorway to the future world, as long ago wise men came to an ordinary stable to seek the birth of the future.

> *Earth has many a noble city;*
> *Bethlehem thou dost all excel:*
> *Out of thee the Lord from heaven*
> *Came to rule his Israel.*
>
> Prudentius

The Vitamin Counter

Sometimes, if you wish to discover the humour and sadness and illogicallity of being a member of the human race, the best place to look is in a mirror.

It is Friday and summer is ending. The first change of the light, the first chill in an evening breeze, says that summer is not for ever. I am in the large department store. I came here to buy a particular thing in the hardware department. I have already got that, but I am now wandering around aimlessly, in that vulnerable way which large department stores encourage, so that I will buy something on impulse.

Suddenly I am in front of a counter that offers me a vast display of vitamins. Everything is designed to tempt me. The word *special* is scattered here and there, each vitamin piled in its own vivid color to appeal to the child inside me. Every bottle looks almost as if it is about to burst with the throbbing nourishment and vitality it claims to contain. I develop a fantasy of myself transfigured, eyes brighter, skin radiant, muscles rippling, sleeping soundly, appearing at the breakfast table in high good humour, setting a cracking pace on the jogging track.

My hand goes forward, not to buy of course but just being curious. There is munchy orange flavoured vitamin C. I shall with its help never again even sneeze. There is yeast extract. I shall surely live to be 95. Here is vitamin D. My bones will stop crackling. So I begin to think to myself that perhaps there is no harm in trying a few of these wonderful things, because there must be something in them. By this time I have as much chance of withdrawal as a fly in a spider's web.

So there they stand on the lazy susan in the kitchen, a row of small bottles, mute witnesses to the eternal hope and gullibility of my anxious and vulnerable humanity.

Why do you spend your money for that which is not bread. . . ?
Isaiah 55:2

The Faces of Love

The other evening I had cause to go to a local store late, to pick up the things that tend to be remembered at odd times — milk, bread, that sort of thing. As is commonplace today to see, set coyly among the endless bric-a-brac of our myriad desires, there were the various best-selling sex magazines.

For some reason one began to realize again the wisdom of the Greeks in having a richer vocabulary for our sexuality than merely one overcrowded English word — *love*. The Greeks spoke of *eros*, from which of course comes "erotic," but they also spoke of *filia*, which essentially means "fellowship." Beyond those words the Greeks used the lovely and indeed terrifying word *agape*.

As I stood there, I began to recall some lines of Matthew Arnold in which he speaks of the gentleness and the tranquility of merely being together, not denying eros but giving it many other levels.

> Only — but this is rare —
> When a beloved hand is laid in ours,
> When, jaded with the rush and glare
> Of the interminable hours,
> Our eyes can in another's eyes read clear
> When our world deafened ear
> Is by the tones of a loved voice caressed —
> A bolt is shot back somewhere in our breast,
> And a lost pulse of feeling starts again;
> The eye sinks inward, and the heart lies plain,
> And what we mean we say, and what
> we would we know,
> And we become aware of our life's flow.

The lines had stayed in my mind from university days. As I looked along the covers of the sex magazines, I thought again of how timeless was the face of everyone of them. They were of course the faces of different young women. In reality they were all renderings of the timeless woman whose name has been in ancient time and in half forgotten places Diana, Astarte, Artemis.

> *Come, my Joy, my Love, my Heart;*
> *Such a Joy as none can move,*
> *Such a Love as none can part,*
> *Such a Heart as joys in love.*   George Herbert

Streets

A Dream of Cities

I have often thought it sad that most religious traditions in our plural society are celebrated and thought about and expressed in a private and almost cult way. Each tradition, whether it be Jewish or Christian or Sikh or Buddhist or Islamic, feels the pressure of a large plural society's wariness, a wariness of particular histories or particular observances.

It is sad that the procession as a religious act is largely absent from today's large western city. It is almost impossible to have an occasion when the costumes and vestments, the symbols and banners and vessels of a tradition, are shown, and men and women and children of that tradition can walk publicly.

I am not naive enough to fail to realize that in past centuries the religious procession has been used as a display of power. But I would hope that in a very plural society that is no longer possible. I dream therefore of a certain situation.

I dream of a city where all men and women would feel free, at a particular season of significance for them, to process as a community of faith, sharing for the occasion the particular symbols and songs by which they express their story and with which they conduct their spiritual journey. I would see a special Way or area, a place somewhere in the city where this could be done. It would not be thought of as a political act, or as one of proselytizing or power play or protest, but merely as the celebration of the community's identity in a very varied city. In the city of my dream such a custom would help all, whatever their mode of belief or unbelief might be, to realize the true riches that they possess in their city.

Let the peoples praise thee, O God; let all the peoples praise thee!
Psalm 67:3

The Wounded Ones

Today in any large city there is moving to and fro a vast and, for the most part, almost invisible minority who are seldom even acknowledged. The fact that they move among the city crowds at all is one of the achievements of our generation. Who are they? It is hard to answer that in a neat phrase. Let me instead describe the situation.

Once upon a time anyone who became mentally ill in our society was institutionalized. That was, if I may use the rather cold blooded and incidentally very ironic word, the *solution.*

In recent years medication has greatly assisted many of us who are mentally wounded. Now some of us can be helped to the degree that we can function fully in positions of responsibility. Others of us can be helped to the degree that we can at least move about in freedon, even if we may not be able to accept responsibility. For a few there will be problems that affect others. Sometimes there are lapses into confusion and anger, frustration or fear. Sometimes medication is not taken, and there are painful consequences.

Whatever the extent of freedom and function that medication can give, I think it important for us to realize that we daily meet our wounded fellow human beings in buses, in libraries, in churches, in restaurants. Sometimes our own fears can trigger in us fear of them, or we can become angry or even feel revulsion. Yet if we think twice, we realize that we inhabit with them a common situation. We are all to a greater or lesser extent wounded by the world we live in. I have not told you anything new. But some things need to be said from time to time.

Go out quickly into the streets and lanes of the city, and bring in the poor and maimed and blind and lame. Luke 14:21

The Stranger

He stands at one of the main intersections of the city. He is there very often and in all kinds of weather. He stands quite still. He is not old. He holds in his hand a religious picture, and from his wrist there usually hangs a long crucifix. You notice as you pass that people tend to walk around him. Nobody, at least to my knowledge, speaks to him. His eyes are deep, his face thin and sometimes pinched from wind or rain or cold.

What is it about such a situation that makes us detour or hesitate or hurry on? I realize that there are surface reasons. Children are taught not to speak to strangers — that sort of thing. But as I look at him, I think there is something deeper.

In the long history of society, and especially in days when men and women clearly understood that the divine acts through all human experience, people often saw unusual appearance or speech or action as significant. They did not dismiss it as strange, but they asked what it was that such and such a demeanour or action was saying.

When I pass this intersection where all the life and activity of a great city meet, where shiny goods are displayed for sale, where towers soar and power structures are represented, where in all this I see a solitary hand holding a dangling crucifix, it makes, however inarticulately or strangely, a timeless statement. It says that at the heart of all life there is inescapably a cross of some kind, that the quality of all the activity and all the powers and all the pulsing world of the city are judged by the quality of him who once hung on a long-ago cross.

He was despised and rejected by men; . . . as one from whom men hid their faces. . . .Isaiah 53:3

Four-Thirty

It was the Friday of a long weekend. The world was moving from one mood to another. The week was ending in long fall shadows between the buildings. I sat at an intersection trying to distinguish the shade of a traffic light that had got lost in the blaze of an evening sunset. I was first in the line.

There were many people coming out of many buildings, brought to earth in their tens of thousands by a thousand sinking elevators. They came out blinking and narrowing their eyes a little as they came.

Then she came. I don't know why I noticed her. She was a young girl, and I have no clear recollection of her, except to say that she registered with me not because of beauty or glamour or sexuality. She was about twenty, and her hair was long and fair in a nondescript way, and she wore a dress. As she came out, she stood for a moment and looked up and around her, as if tasting the air and the sky. Then she walked a few steps to the sidewalk and stopped, took off her cardigan, and slung it over her shoulder. She shook her hair back and set out across the street. Half way across she stopped again, bent down, and took her shoes off. Holding them in her hand she bounded across the other lanes and reached the sidewalk. She moved swiftly and gracefully, her hair flashing in the sun until she was lost in the crowds.

Long after she had gone, her image stayed in my mind. Everything about her seemed to be a celebration of joy and life and freedom.

. . . ye shall go out with joy, and be led forth with peace.
Isaiah 55:12

Lovers

A new hospital has been built and the street has been widened. There is now a traffic island which helps when one is crossing. That is important, because here in this particular place there is needed a sensitivity to people for a particular reason.

It is raining as I turn left off the side street onto the wide boulevard. Ahead of me on the gleaming black surface, I see her crossing. She is walking very slowly because there are now more years than there used to be. I know where she is going and what she will do. She is dressed neatly and attractively for her age, because she is the kind of person who knows that these things are important. She has ample reason to have become careless. She has been coming here for a long time. She will go down familiar corridors and take familiar elevators. When the two of them meet, they will not say a great deal. That will not mean they are not (as we say these days) communicating. Since they have shared a long past, much now flows silently from all that shared experience. There have been a few children, another country, war, some happiness, no great wealth, sickness that came at first intermittently and now is permanent.

If I pass this place later in the afternoon or early evening, I may see her heading home again. If I hailed her, she would not only smile but — such is her nature — she would laugh. She would laugh more if I were to say that she, and others like her, are what that often misused phrase "great lovers" really means. Theirs is a loving, both of life and of another human being, that possesses great resilience and faithfulness. How often greatness and nobility of spirit stand in the rain waiting for traffic to go by.

Love bears all things, believes all things, hopes all things, endures all things. 1 Corinthians 13:7

One Flesh

I sometimes wish that there was a machine that could photograph a moment of humanity in words as instantaneously as we can do it on film. A machine that could hold and preserve the mixture of rich images that enter the mind when one not only sees a face or an action or a passing gesture but sees meanings beyond each of them.

It was a holiday and around lunch time. The streets were fairly empty, almost drowsy. The air was shot through with the thinning yellow light of spring sunshine.

Across the intersection they walked very slowly. It was not because they were old or infirm. They were a young couple, both, I would say, in their early twenties. She was in the last month of pregnancy, and walked with that deliberation needed to balance her body against its unaccustomed weight. Her face, which was a lovely face, had that fine drawn look that pregnancy can bring, the skin tending to a transparency, as if her whole being by nature was orientated inward for the task of forming this new life.

They were touching slightly, not at this time speaking, as if a light touch were now sufficient speech. There was about them a kind of primitive quality set amid all the chic clothes shops and svelte hotels. In their faces and their stillness, there seemed, even as they moved, a fulfillment of love rather than merely a satiation of passion. I suppose that, above all, their significance lay in the fact that they were living out the great natural and eternal cycle of life and love.

"Have you never read that the Creator made them from the beginning male and female?" Jesus added, "For this reason a man shall leave his father and mother, and be made one with his wife; and the two shall become one flesh."

The Contract

At night the centre of a large city seems like a checkerboard of light and darkness. The intense sources of light from cars and traffic lights and lighted windows makes the areas of shadow appear deeper by contrast. Because of this crossplay of light and darkness, all life and its movements are heightened. There is a flash of eyes, the turning of a face suddenly there and then gone, a constant moving from light to darkness and from darkness to light.

I am walking from the cathedral, along the blocks where very often cold and rain-drenched people offer one their company for a certain price. They offer it according to their personality in ways that vary from the whispered and the furtive to the brash and good humoured. Across the street two police motorcycles reflect the lights on their gleaming chrome.

As I come along the block, an arrangement is being made. Both the man and the woman are very young, probably in their early twenties. In the few moments in which this urban cameo is played out, one cannot help noticing a lot of things. There is the extraordinary joylessness of it all. There is the approach, on one side tense and tentative, on the other bored, speculative, detached. The faces are lifeless as they discuss something that is given to us as the most vital and intoxicating of our human experiences.

After the short interchange of arranging they turn to walk away. I very nearly said "together." But that is the very quality that is so terribly absent. They walk apart, together in a contract but basically alienated. They do not speak. There is not even the simple human gesture of a touch of hands. There is a meeting, yet no meeting, an intended intimacy without any intimacy whatsoever. Where there is supposed to be life and joy there is a kind of deadness and non-feeling. It is a pathetic charade of such a profound reality.

If I have not love, I gain nothing. 1 Corinthians 13:3

Construction Site

The downtown area has a huge scar of excavations scattered through it. Some day from these vast excavations, towering structures will emerge to grace the city. At the moment they do not grace anything. They look like all construction sites.

At first the great machines tear the earth and dump it into great trucks which grind along the streets while mere mortals pay them respect. Then the concrete and steel begins to fill the great hole. Sparks flash as the welders work. Slowly the huge spine of the construction crane rises, until it stands like a gigantic gaunt bird swinging its head to and fro with titbits for the waiting workmen. At night floodlights illuminate the cold glittering chaos that lies behind the grubby mudstained scaffolding and the grey steel fence.

Yet the human scene is so full of contrasts. Against all I have just described, I see one day a family scene. For some reason one of the men in his hard hat has been called to the gate by his family. His wife is telling him something. There are two small children. He has one in his arms, and the child is tugging at his father's hard hat. The man is smiling at his wife; so I presume that the news is good. But it strikes me as a door opening into a world we so often understand as hard and tough and unfeeling, a world of power, of technology, of union-management struggle. Sometimes a construction site seems synonymous with all that soulessness and hostility. We even use the term "hard hat" to express those very things.

Yet the hands of a child reach for a hard hat in the shadow of all the machines. They find a parent's love. A family makes an island of humanity as the city pours by on either side. I felt that I had glimpsed something of God in the city of humanity.

. . . I make you hear new things, hidden things which you have not known. Isaiah 48:6

Butterfly

It was a golden noonhour, the streets filling with the crowds of office people and tourists. Men from offices in shirts and ties, men wearing open shirts or no shirts at all, women with summer dresses and brown skin and shining hair — the human race undergoing that subtle change that comes with summer and the sun. Little restaurants had their doors wide open, and some had placed a few tables on the sidewalk in joyous defiance of law and practicality.

In this fleeting golden noon as I turned the crowded corner, I saw it move down the street with grace and beauty, shimmering in the sun as it turned this way and that. It was about a foot above the heads of us giants with whom it shared the earth, and it seemed to be searching first one way and then the other. I wondered where its lost home was. In some quiet West End garden or in what must seem to such a tiny creature the great green universe of Stanley Park. I wondered why it had left and wandered into this cacophonous concrete world of many dangers.

Its wings were rich and deep in colour, varied and beautiful and fragile. I watched it set out across the great roaring gulf of the wide downtown street. As it did so, a huge truck braked to a halt at the light, its thundering and shuddering engine high above those who stood at the crossing. The butterfly was caught in the whirlwind of this steel goliath, caught by the heat and currents of power. Its wings faltered for a moment. It fluttered lower. It seemed bound for the chaos of human feet and machine wheels of the crowded street.

Then it rallied. It rose above the great shuddering radiator, above the trembling mirror and the driver's window, and then it leapt again into the air and soared swiftly up and up beyond the corner of the public library. I looked until I saw a last flash of beating wings, and then it was gone.

He has made everything beautiful in its time. . . . Ecclesiastes 3:11

The Artist

The other day I watched somebody at work downtown. I meant only to glance, but I found that I was held. I became aware of a skill that I had never known before. Perhaps I had known it in an unthinking way, but I became aware of it now for the first time. You could describe this scene in everyday language and forget about it. All I saw was a man operating a mechanical digger. But you could also describe it in other language. I was looking at a very gifted craftsmen at work.

The machine was below me in the excavation, and it was huge. At its heart he sat, hard-hatted, seemingly tiny. In front of him lay the shale and dust and stones, the layers of time exposed in the busy modern city. In front of him the huge arm of the machine soared, bisecting down to the great claw. By his hand were the black-topped levers. Here were his instruments, the glistening keyboard on which he played a music of motion, the brushes with which he painted designs on the rock wall as the machine bit into it. His hands moved minimally like a highly disciplined conductor getting great power from an orchestra with almost imperceptible signs. The vast machine edged forward, the arms swung in a perfectly judged arc, the claws broke, swept, gathered, lifted, and dropped the load with perfect precision.

I thought again of a conductor, a piano player. But he also brought to my mind the image of a surgeon wielding an instrument, in this case massive, but wielding it with as much grace as a surgeon does. We are slow to see beauty in technology, grace in the mechanical, poetry in the city. It was a thrilling glimpse of an artist in hard hat.

> *God of concrete, God of steel,*
> *God of piston and of wheel*
> *God of atom, God of mine:*
> *All the world of power is thine.*
>
> Richard Granville Jones

The Photograph

There is traffic on the bridge at this evening hour, lots of it. It thunders homeward on this sunny evening. Light is everywhere in a high soaring blue-domed world. The water shimmers out past the planetarium and on into the wide expanse of the bay. Up and down the sidewalks of the bridge the illegal and inevitable bicycles move.

There in the middle of the moving and shining universe they stand. He is elderly as, indeed, is she. They have decided to take a photograph. Perhaps while passing by in some city tour bus, they made the decision and walked back here from the hotel. He stands against the wall of the bridge. The homespun trousers ill-fitting over black boots; shirt and tie framed between shoulder suspenders. Scant grey hair is flying in the light breeze. The face is puckered by age and light; it is healthily coloured at the moment by vacation, and probably by life on a farm. She is taking great trouble to get the correct position, to place him in this context of city highrises and blue ocean. I can watch them as the traffic halts me in its line. As I move away, they are still there, preparing to fix him in that frame for years to come.

For all I know there is a certain anxiety to get it right because health may be failing and this may be a special holiday. This photograph will eventually be shared and smiled over. It will become the stuff of memory. It will be exchanged among a generation or two. It will perhaps be treasured by someone. Taking it is a kind of lovemaking. It is a capturing of eyes, a keeping of a beloved face and smile. It is saying that somebody matters, that they are unique, that they are loved. The scene lingered in my mind as I drove on.

Wondrously show thy steadfast love, . . . Keep me as the apple of the eye. . . . Psalm 17:7–8

A Prestige Place

I am intrigued by the devices used by the advertising world to lure us to do this or that, to buy this or that, to live here or there. Somewhere in the cellars of their agencies they must keep pet psychiatrists, trained for the trade's needs, chained to desks and forced to reveal all the human traits that can be exploited to motivate our basest instincts. For the most part it works, unless you hesitate before rushing out to buy.

The other day my eyes lit on what was called a prestige advertisement. That is a much beloved word in the trade. The product, an apartment block, was prestige; the district was prestige. The presumption being made was that all the buyers, presumably your potential neighbours, would without exception be prestige. Even the print and layout were classical, slim, restrained — again prestige! What you were meant to believe is that, if you could get the hideous amount of money together, you too would end up being impeccably prestige.

What do they say in the ad? "For people," they cry, "who take luxury, security, and privacy for granted." I am sure when the writer had coined that ringing phrase he savoured it, swung his chair back, tried it for sound on the chandelier, and then took it proudly to the next executive in line. But, just think about it. Do you wish to be the kind of person who takes luxury and security and privacy for granted?

First, luxury. If you really do take that for granted, I pity you, poor jaded joyless mortal you must be. Privacy. If you take that for granted you are very probably missing one of the few things that give joy and life in today's world, the varied ebb and flow of ages and sexes, faces and voices that share your life with you in so many ways. If you take security for granted then you are indeed a deluded soul. I seem to remember an old story in an old book, a story about a man who decided to build bigger barns, probably very prestige, and God said, perhaps in a dream, but that is just as effective coming from God, "You fool . . . " God said a little more, but I imagine that was quite enough.

. . . God said to him, Fool! This night your soul is required of you. . . . Luke 12:20

The New Jews

It could have been any day. It was late morning. The traffic was heavy, the city was now going about its business. I was part of that traffic, part of that business.

I suddenly saw them. I think the reason why they first caught my eye is that there were whole family groups together. I think also it is because they were dressed rather formally. For a moment I was curious. Then I noticed the white circular headcovering on some of the men, and I realized that I was driving in the area of the synagogue and that these folk were Jewish families emerging and returning home from a religious observance. Thinking afterwards I am almost certain that it was the observance of the Day of Atonement, but at the moment that is not important.

As I drove on, I could not help but reflect on something quite new that has entered in to western life. For centuries all through our culture Jewish folk have had to observe their faith outside the normal rhythm of society. They have had to ask their children to make choices that are not easy for children to make, to worship when others played, to observe things that others did not observe, to be different.

For generations it has been very different for Christians. When they worshipped, the world closed down. Religion for their children meant conformity and acceptance, not difference. But as society changes and becomes more secular, as Christian observance becomes a choice rather than a social convention, as Christians cease to depend on the surrounding culture to pass on their tradition — as all this happens, an interesting thing is taking place. Christians are beginning to experience at least some elements of the centuries-long Jewish experience, of having to appear to be different, of having to make choices about priorities, of having to find a way to pass on their symbols and tradition to the new generation.

As I reflected I felt very near to those families walking home or to their cars, having worshipped God as the world passed by.

When in time to come your son asks you, 'What does this mean?' you will say to him, 'By strength of hand the Lord brought us out of Egypt. . . . ' Exodus 13:14

Altar

Hands

Centuries ago, Albrecht Durer painted a pair of hands. They are fineboned and sensitive hands, worn and yet graceful. They are clasped in the traditional attitude of prayer. Durer's "Praying Hands" as the painting is often called, will probably remain as long as the culture that we know remains.

I found myself thinking of those fine and striking hands when somebody, with whom I had shared a liturgy, expressed an insight that had come to him for the first time.

In recent years, among the many changes that have come in Christian worship, is that of lay participation. For a thousand years in many traditions, among them my own, all things in liturgy or worship have been done by the priest or priests. But today much of that is changed, and the liturgy resembles a drama (which it really is) in which parts are played by many actors.

Among these are the men and women who come forward from the congregation at a certain moment in the Mass or Eucharist. They are then given the chalices of wine and the ciboria containing bread. These they distribute to everyone else. In this particular Eucharist one of the ministers of bread is, for most of his working hours, a surgeon. When for the first time he had given the sacred bread to more than two hundred people, placing it in their hands and saying simply, "the body of Christ," he was awed by the experience. Even though this man was so used to the sight of human limbs, what filled him with awe was the infinite variety of hands upstretched to receive the divine yet simple gift. To his sensitive eyes every pair of hands told a story, each embodied a mystery. It was moving to see in his eyes and to hear in his voice the awe of that discovery.

Lift up your hands to the holy place, and bless the Lord!
Psalm 134:2

A Forgotten Family

Here is a sad story that is not about any one person but about an increasing number of people. It takes place every day in every large city.

Mrs Smith is elderly and lives alone. For many years she has been active and sociable. One of the things she has always been active in is, let's call it, St Peter's Church. St Peter's could be of any tradition anywhere. Here two things have happened. She has had a life-long faith strengthened and affirmed by worship and prayer and sacrament. She has become part of a community. Sometimes Mrs Smith has been in other homes of that church community, and perhaps a group of familiar faces and voices of St Peter's have been in her apartment. When Mrs Smith was sick, a few people from St Peter's dropped in. Sometimes if Mrs Smith was downtown to see a doctor or something, she would drop in and say hello at St Peter's because it was one of the places that felt like home.

So Mrs Smith becomes very old and very sick and she dies. Into the airport an individual or a couple fly from a thousand miles away. They know nobody in town, and since they have only exchanged Christmas cards with Mrs Smith, they know nothing, or at least very little, of her life. Sadly enough this holds true sometimes, although they may be members of Mrs Smith's family.

Even though somebody from St Peter's may have an opportunity to tell them how much her faith and her community meant, they themselves may not share that faith. Mrs Smith may even have said that she would wish her body to be brought to the place where she had found community and faith. That too can be seen as irrelevant by an impatient visitor. So the matter of Mrs Smith's death is dealt with. What is important is that it has not been dealt with as an aspect, and as an integral part, of her life. I think that's sad.

How lovely is thy dwelling place, O Lord of hosts! My soul longs, yea, faints for the courts of the Lord; . . . Psalm 84: 1,2

The Medicine of Truth

It is fascinating to see how many of the therapies of our time have much in common, although their language seems to differ.

For instance, it is a commonplace of our decade to say that what we are thinking about is very much connected with, and very much affects, our general health. That insight, which is really a very old one, is expressed today by many therapies, some linked to eastern symbols and traditions, others linked to Christian spirituality, still others communicated in various ways by counsellors, therapists, psychologists.

We are all only too aware that the reality we live in is full of much ugliness, darkness, fear, anxiety, and other shadowed things. We are also aware that we do not deal with them adequately by trying to anaesthetize ourselves against them. But I think it worthwhile to try to express as often as possible those elements of life that at best strengthen us, and give us a sense of beauty or goodness, or indeed even make us smile.

That short simple reflection emerges from a passage in one of St Paul's long ago letters. Probably Paul's words in turn come from some Greek poet or philosopher of his time.

> Whatsoever things are true,
> whatsoever things are honest,
> whatsoever things are just,
> whatsoever things are pure,
> whatsoever things are lovely,
> whatsoever things are of good report,
> if there be any virtue,
> and if there be any praise,
> think on these things.

After twenty centuries it's still a very good idea, don't you think.

Ancient Encounter

Recently I watched a very interesting and, I think, significant thing take place. At a certain stage in the combined meetings of the Canadian and Australian Medical Associations, about five hundred doctors were sitting in the cathedral, taking part in the honouring of various people and appointing and installing their particular officers.

I was given a few moments to speak, and having welcomed them, I couldn't help saying that I thought I saw a significance in the occasion. I felt that we, priest and physician, were meeting once again in the sanctuary from which we both once emerged. For centuries, indeed probably millennia, the functions of priest and physician were blended. It is significant that the very name of that function was not a word that meant *curer* but the lovely and ancient word *healer*.

That word is in turn related to another —, the word *whole*. To heal is to make whole again. One of the moments in history when we see very clearly the ancient blending of things, now seen as very much apart, is in a Jewish context. In Judaism the gift of healing was seen as that of many people. When Jesus healed a person of one of the many skin conditions that come under the old biblical word *leprosy*, he sometimes directed the person to a priest. Then the priest would pronounce the person healed or whole again.

In that ancient world you are dealing with another sense of wholeness — the fact that life itself was seen as a whole. Body, mind, spirit were thought of as blended together in a single entity. But that changed. I suspect that in some ways we are the poorer for the change. I notice there are signs abroad of our trying to recover what was true in that ancient synthesis.

For thou didst form my inward parts . . . my frame was not hidden from thee when I was being made in secret . . . .
Psalm 139: 13,15

The Christian Feasts

The phone rang and it was somebody from one of the newspapers. They were doing a feature on what they had decided to call "the January syndrome." I don't know what the author eventually called it, but that's what it was to be about when it all emerged on the features page. It would be an article on the phenomenon of post Christmas and New Year blues, the reason for them and the ways people deal with them.

As we talked about the strange phenomenon of modern holidays, we found ourselves remembering some very old and timeless things. Almost all our modern urban holidays are based on a much older rural cycle. The thing about that old cycle is that the holiday was not merely a single frantic day or possibly crowded weekend. It was a season. There was a time of preparation.

You see this most obviously in the cycle of the Christian year which we inherited from about the fifth century. In that rhythm Christmas is not a day but a season. There is a period of anticipation called Advent, and there is a long period for the echoes to be heard dying away, for savouring its meaning and its symbols. That period we call Epiphany.

Now all that may seem nothing more than ancient ecclesiastical information, but it is much more. Psychologically it is far wiser than the emotional explosion we call Christmas today. There is in the old cycle anticipation, enjoyment, recollection. For us today there is no time for anticipation. There is a rather frantic and determined enjoyment and almost no recollection. This is because the atmosphere and the music and the symbols of it all are abruptly swept away and silenced.

So I found myself saying to my newspaper friend that we used to celebrate Christmas, and indeed all seasons, organically, in a natural rhythm with life. Today we celebrate everything orgasmically, with all the seeming ecstasy of that but, of course, with its cost in emotional exhaustion.

. . . teach us to number our days that we may get a heart of wisdom. Psalm 90:12

Time Limit

A few days before Good Friday the television people rang up. They said that they wanted to do a piece on the evening news about the meaning of Good Friday and Easter Sunday. I asked them how much of a time slot we had, and they said about three minutes. So a little later we met at the church and they set up a camera. I tried in about three hundred words to state the central mystery of the Christian faith.

We now move to Good Friday morning itself. The phone rings again. This time it is another television station, and they have suddenly decided that they would like someone to do a short statement on the meaning of Good Friday and Easter. Once again I ask the essential question in the land of television, How long have we got? The answer this time was two minutes. When the crew arrive, I ask them how long have we really got? The answer is one minute. So in one minute we try to state the essentials of the Easter mystery.

After you do that, you feel you have betrayed the faith because of what you *haven't* said. It was only a few days later however, while a few hundred people were saying the creed in the middle of the Eucharist, that I realized I had been doing something that men and women in the third and fourth centuries would have perfectly understood.

They said to themselves that they simply had to find ways of expressing the essentials of the Christian faith in a very short statement. So they put together what became the great creeds of history, beginning with the deceptively simple language we find so familiar in the Apostles' Creed and later in the Nicene Creed. Somebody wrote, "I believe in one God, maker of heaven and earth, and of all things visible and invisible."

One man who had a great deal to do with forming the Nicene Creed was Athanasius. He lived in the fourth century, but he would have been quite at home with the clock-watching demands of today's radio and television stations.

. . .be ready always to give an answer to every man that asketh you a reason of the hope that is in you. . . . 1 Peter 3:15

Religious Symbols

As we in western society move into the reality of being a plural society, we are going to have to come to terms with what is in the western world, at least for the majority of its people, a new problem of living together. It is simple to state and not at all so simple to live up to. More and more we are going to have to find a way of acknowledging and living with the validity of each other's religious symbols.

One way we will be tempted to do this is for religious symbols to be banished to the private worlds of the personal, the home, the place of religious gathering. That sounds a safe and reasonable device until you realize that the cost would be impoverishing for all. A whole dimension of life, some would say the deepest dimension of life, would be sadly unshareable.

Suppose for a moment we are in another galaxy far away. Suppose the ultimate value of that civilization is what we call music. Suppose that in time music becomes so rich among them that there are innumerable kinds of it. So on that galaxy they decide that this problem will be dealt with by removing all music from public life, public utterance, public occasions. Privately it may be enjoyed, also in secluded groups. But it may not be acknowledged by the community as a whole. How sad and foolish that would be. Yet we are tending to deal with the religious dimension of life in that very way in our society.

Seek the Lord while he may be found, call upon him while he is near. . . . Isaiah 55:6

No Short Cuts

One of the most obvious features of the last decade is the degree to which, in spite of Rudyard Kipling, East and West have met. Many voices have said how rich in religious insight the East is and how poverty stricken the West has become. The religions of the East have affected us in passingly cultural ways such as the use of the word *guru*, now almost a slang term for "guide," and in very fundamental ways such as the formation of Hare Khrishna or Divine Light communities.

This search for enlightenment from the East is part of an even greater movement, in the last fifteen years or so, which has seen millions of people in the West seeking for innumerable awarenesses to what I call self-development or self-realization. To respond to that longing there have sprung up equally innumerable techniques, programs, institutions, paperbacks, cassette tapes — all to some degree promising the longed-for self-realization. In a sentence, we have seen many examples of things good in themselves, with a long and great history behind them, simplified, attractively packaged, and pushed on the self-development market.

I was aware of this again recently when I was reading Thomas Merton's *Asian Journal*, a record of the last journey he made in his continuing efforts to build bridges between his own Catholic Christian tradition and Buddhist traditions. I was aware of the life-long self-discipline he had brought to that search, the endless study, the long dialogues conducted with great figures of the East, among them the Dalai Lama. Even then Merton confessed himself only on the edge of a great ocean of both self-discovery and the discovery of God. I became aware again of how we vulgarize the search for self and God when we promise it in a quickie paperback, a long weekend, or a course of lectures "six for the price of five," paid in advance. It isn't that easy.

Lord, who shall abide in thy tabernacle? who shall dwell in thy holy hill? Psalm 15:1

Dalai Lama

We had been honoured by a visit from the Dalai Lama. At a certain stage of the visit of His Holiness, there was a simple action that involved everyone in the cathedral. There were assembled approximately a thousand men, women, and children of all the world's main religious traditions. Each had been given a candle. At a certain moment a number of men and women representing the various faiths went among the people with lighted candles. I had not expected the Dalai Lama to wish to do this, yet he immediately and spontaneously did, moving hither and yon, lighting a candle here and there, leaning across to an eager child, laughing when he couldn't ignite the flame on a candle the first time — generally being a problem to his bodyguards who were endeavouring to be discreet about their role.

As he moved here and there, eyes gleaming with enjoyment, smiling, and laughing, I couldn't help but become aware of an immense dignity that didn't need to be dignified, a sense so deep of the majesty and mystery of life that one didn't have to be either majestic or mysterious. Here was a wisdom secure enough that it didn't have to seem solemn but could almost seem to play the fool.

Long ago St Paul spoke about being a fool for Christ. It is a quality not many of us are great enough or good enough or spiritual enough to possess. I suspect that Francis of Assisi had it. In our lifetime John XXIII certainly did. Francis and his friends were called "God's jesters." It is a lovely phrase. As I watched the Dalai Lama, I knew that I had met one of God's great jesters.

. . . the foolishness of God is wiser than men . . . .
1 Corinthians 1:25

Skull Cap

Actions, so they say, speak louder than words. I know that as do you, but from time to time experiencing it brings it home, sometimes in very simple ways.

I received an invitation to hear Marc Tanenbaum. He is a rabbi whose work and whose brilliance have made him a world figure in Judaism. In recent years he has been involved in a commission that meets with the West German government to work out final decisions about the statute of limitations on the responsibility for war crimes. To hear Marc Tanenbaum I received an invitation to a nearby synagogue.

As I went up the steps to the entrance to the synagogue and turned to enter the seating area, a person welcomed me, handed me the small black skull cap which all men entering the synagogue wear, and asked me to put it on. I did so, at first unthinkingly, or no more so than considering it good manners to conform as an invited guest in someone else's sacred place. But as I sat there, feeling this simple thing on my head, I suddenly began to realize how often throughout a long history the wearing of that cap (it is called a Yarmulka) had cost so much in ridicule, hatred, persecution, even death. It was as if, by this simple act of donning the Yarmulka, I experienced something such as we experience when we put a shell to our ear. I seemed to hear the sound of a great ocean of tradition and faith. Across its endless generations there were mingled pain and suffering and beauty.

When I returned the Yarmulka at the end of the evening, I realized again the power of a God who speaks to us through simple things.

These are they who have come out of the great tribulation. . . . Rev. 7:14

Kristallnacht

The stage of the large synagogue is simply arranged. In front of the small group of people on the platform is a table. On the table are six candles. The setting is simple and stark.

In the course of the evening twelve people are called from the congregation. Six of them are elderly; six are young adults. They come forward, a young adult lifts the candle, an older person lights it. They replace it on the table and step aside. One by one the candles are lifted, lit, replaced. Once again the small table stands centre stage. We all look at it, the six tiny flames rising and falling in their glass containers. There is silence across the very large crowd.

The candles? They have significance, immense significance. Each one represents one million men, women, and children — one million dead men and women and children. The six candles represent six million Jewish dead. Each of the older men and women have one thing in common. They have survived. Each have been present on the night of 9 November 1938 when Europe first heard the sound of shouts and jackboots and shattered glass and screams.

They call it Kristallnacht, from the long-ago shattered glass. It is recalled here in this vivid and poignant ceremony. The words said and sung do not need to be in a familiar language. They communicate a remembered agony. But the candles are also lit this night in hope. Hope that the sound of broken glass will not again be heard and that the fires will not again be lit and humanity will not again discover its own terrible darkness.

. . . dogs are round about me; a company of evildoers encircle me . . . they stare and gloat over me; . . . O Lord, be not far off! . . . hasten to my aid! Psalm 22: 16, 19

Laboratory

A Hidden Spirituality

How much has the world changed in the last twenty-five years? More precisely, how much has our western world changed?

If you wish to find the answer, pick up what can be a fascinating cross-section of the average contempory mind. It is, as far as I know, usually free. It is the course list of all that is being offered in any university centre for continuing education. If you glance at some of the courses, you see the great changes that have occurred in western society's consciousness.

The page of science courses is very far from the technological show-and-tell of the 1950s. Here is a science no longer thinking of itself as the whole of things but only a part, seeing itself as subject rather than object, as caring, as part of a total ecology. Turn to philosophy. It is now sought not merely as analytical and cerebral but as potentially healing and therapeutic. Look at life styles. Here again the emphasis is on the therapeutic. To the fore are our dreams, our stress, our loneliness. Turn to almost any page, and you will discover a deep sense of wonder about the human predicament, a deep sense of caring about the stages of human growth, an awareness of the fragility of the environment in which we live.

The supreme irony is that in the list of courses there is almost no religion in any official stated organized way. Ironically the world you see in these pages is quite obviously embarked on a mystical and spiritual search unknown to more officially religious generations.

. . . the whole creation has been groaning in travail together until now; and not only the creation, but we ourselves . . . .
Romans 8:23

84

Meeting Place

I see that that renowned figure in genetics, David Susuki, was recently speaking from a stage shared with one of our national symphonies. He was expressing the hope that science and philosophy could be joined as we move into the future.

Many realize that such cooperation is vitally necessary. I think it is already happening, but it will not be easy. So far these two children of the West have found it difficult to see in one another what each needs. There seems to be an inevitable tendency for one to grow far beyond the other, then to dismiss the other as either evil or contemptible.

In the Middle Ages philosophy and its sister theology fascinated and fully engaged the western mind. At the edges of society were those engaged in an embryonic pursuit called science. They were viewed as at worst evil and at best harmless. Then a huge tidal wave of history broke. Renaissance and reformation shattered one world and began to mould another. Over four or five centuries this new world has grown until positions have become reversed. Up to our lifetime the physical sciences, bestriding human life, engaged the admiration, the energy, even the reverence of a whole civilization. On the edge have been philosohpers, theologians, poets, visionaries. They have been seen as at best quaintly fascinating and at worst destructively critical. Recently however, as the 1980s move on, the imbalance of four centuries begins to be questioned. Such is the nature of time and history, the fact that the question is now even being asked means that the shift has already begun.

What, one longs to know, will be the shape of the next chapter in the stormy relationship between the laboratory and the temple?

. . . in him all things were created . . . through him and for him.
Colossians 1:16,17

The New Dialogue

A new meeting is taking place; In the last few years a new conversation has begun. The scientist and the public are beginning, only just beginning, to meet. It isn't yet happening on a broad scale, and it isn't easy for the scientific world to enter into public discussion. The instinct of the scientist has been to avoid dialogue in favour of a fairly single minded quest for knowledge.

There are other factors that make dialogue anything but easy. For instance, especially in the new field of genetics and microbiology, the physicist and the philosopher, ethicist, and priest are beginning to talk together. Again, it is only beginning, but it is there.

Science and philosphy are uneasy bedfellows, and there are valid reasons. Science is precise, neat, measured. Philosophy, ethics, and faith are not and cannot be any of those things. Again, in today's scientific world things move sometimes very quickly. For faith, ethics, and philosophy there must be time to reflect. Also, when the scientist looks for opinion and direction about the values and morality of his work, he finds that western society no longer speaks only from a Judeo-Christian tradition but from a plural and varied situation. And whereas physics tends to be cumulative — the discoveries of this decade build on those of the last and so on — philosophy and ethics tend to be more immediate. Especially these days we feel that if we are to grapple with the unprecedented questions we face, philosophy and ethics and faith have got to discover again what will address the current situation.

The new dialogue with the physicist is especially difficult because for a long time in the western world the Judeo-Christian tradition involved itself mainly in the private area of human life, the personal. It largely left the great flood of public life to flow undisturbed — science, art, commerce, medicine, urbanization, and all that. So today reopening the conversation between scientist and philosopher is not easy, but it must take place. I'm aware of all that as I sit at a table with five geneticists who are trying to assess the risks of certain procedures.

There is no speech nor language, where their voice is not heard.
Psalm 19:3

Worlds Alive

One of the intriguing things about the human mind is how we often reach intuitively for a great insight years or even centuries before we begin to arrive at it deductively.

I open an issue of *Saturday Review*. There are a number of articles on the theme "God and Science — New Allies." One could reflect for a while on that title and its ironic implication that somehow God has taken this long to recognize the benefits of science, but let that be. In one of those articles there is described the epoch-making change in human thought which is emerging in our time. There is a growing realization that all matter, animate and inanimate, is essentially energy and is therefore in a mysterious sense, alive.

There is no denying the immense significance in that contemporary scientific discovery. Yet listen to this passage, written nearly two thousand years ago by a first century writer in a letter to a community in Rome.

> *The created universe waits with eager expectation. . . The universe was made the victim of frustration, not by its own choice but by him who made it so. . . Yet always there is hope because the universe itself is to be freed from the shackles of mortality. . . Up to the present we know the whole created universe groans in all its parts as if in the pangs of childbirth.*
> Romans 8:22

When St Paul expressed that insight, he was journeying to the bounds of human imagination. In fact, if we believe what we say we believe about the inspiration of those who wrote Holy Scripture, we might say that he was expressing an insight given to him beyond those bounds.

The universe is energy and is totally alive physically, states contemporary science. The universe is the creation of God and is totally alive spiritually, says the first century faith. It is good to place the letter to the Romans beside that issue of *Saturday Review*, and to realize that God communicates the wonder of creation in many ways and in every age.

Alive With Whom?

We sometimes look back at great truths or great changes in the way people thought, insights that changed the world. We feel there must have been some moment when the world changed. I suspect that this is the reason why stories are woven around great human insights. Isaac Newton saw the apple fall, and suddenly he discovered gravity. There is old Archimedes relaxing in his bath. Suddenly he shouts "eureka" because he has just realized Archimedes' Law, jumps out of his bath, and runs off naked to announce to a waiting world whatever that scientific breakthrough was. (Like you I once knew what Archimedes' Principle is but, again probably like you, I've forgotten!)

Yet I think the truth, for most of us, is that great discoveries and great changes sneak quietly up on us. Take something that has been coming more and more clear to scientists as this decade passes. It is so mind-boggling that it seems almost impertinent and ludicrous to try to express it in this moment or two.

Today we are very near to changing for ever the way mankind thinks about matter. For, as we have gained the ability to enter deeper and deeper into the nature of matter, as we have been able to discover smaller and smaller elements of matter, we are beginning to realize that, at its deepest levels, matter merges into energy. Do you realize what that is telling us? If all matter is energy, then there is no distinction between animate and inanimate matter. And that is expressing nothing less than an awe inspiring insight, that in fact the totality of creation is pulsating as energy, in fact that all of creation is alive!

Perhaps the next question is, Alive with what? Maybe we should ask, Alive with whom? That's a question that echoes in the mind.

All things were made by him; and without him was not any thing made that was made. John 1:3

Doctors and Priests

I found myself in a situation that made me realize once again how very much people and society, and indeed the whole human inner world, have changed. It was the evening banquet of a convention in a large hotel. The industry was a major resource industry — natural gas — and the delegates were from across the country.

For twenty minutes or so I tried to deal with the meaning of their industry, the motivations behind what they did in that industry, the things that pressure them, the self-image that they had of themselves. I found myself using two images for their role in society, as men involved in producing natural gas for power, two images that, to put it mildly, would be new to them.

I suggested they consider the role of a doctor. A doctor is one whom we allow to peer and probe into the deepest recess of our bodies. If the planet is being regarded more and more as a living entity, a body, then, I suggested, they in the resources industries are being trusted to probe its deepest recesses. They are then the doctors of the earth, a trust held in their hands.

I then spoke of a priest as one who handles holy things. A priest holds our child for baptism, joins our hands in marriage, handles the sacramental elements. Anyone in the resource industries, anyone producing power from the earth, is doing precisely that, handling the holiness of the earth.

I was very struck by the way in which what I had to say was heard, and by the way it touched chords. Fifteen years ago, at least in my experience, it would have been almost impossible to say such things and to be heard. But today there is a wind of natural spirituality everywhere.

. . . God saw everything that he made, and behold, it was very good.
Genesis 1:31

Cain and Abel

The invitation to address an energy conference was welcome. I found myself speaking of the old story of Cain and Abel, reading it in a modern translation. The text referred to Cain as one who tilled the ground and to Abel as one who tended the sheep. As you recall, Cain murders Abel.

Cain tilled the ground, so the old story says. Do you see how tilling is the opening, the entering, at best the fertilizing, at worst the raping of the earth? It is the male act. Abel on the other hand tends the sheep; his stance is one of caring and preserving. Abel signifies the feminine aspect of existence.

One suddenly realizes a very modern thing about that ancient story. Cain is the symbol of the masculine, Abel of the feminine. If the myth had been born today and not in ancient Babylon, Adam and Eve would in the story have been given a boy and a girl.

This concept is important today because we, as technological humanity, have been Cain in our attitude to the earth. We have moulded, developed, mined, used it. The temptation of Cain is to end up as a murderer. What does the element of Cain in us murder? It wishes to murder the "Abel" in us, the feminine, the part of us that wants to care for the earth and cherish it.

Our struggle today is to balance our stance to technology and nature. How do we get a technology (symbolized by Cain) that is mingled with a caring stance to nature and the environment (symbolized by Abel)? We must somehow find that balance. There are an increasing number of people within the structures of technology, in mining corporations and hydro electric corporations, who are mindful of the need for this balance. The alternative in the ancient story is violence and tragedy.

The earth is the Lord's and the fullness thereof. . . . Psalm 24:1

Planetarium

It was raining and it was a holiday and we decided to go to the planetarium. In a way the planetarium is both very new and very old.

First you go up in the elevator. As you do, you realize that since the dawn of time builders have taken care that worshippers approaching temples must go up. Here in this planetarium the approaches move from the exterior bright light to dimmer light. The passage narrows, glimpses of things to come are on pictures and diagrams on the walls. All these are the equivalents of ancient hieryogliphics and, later on, stained glass windows. The shape of the particular paradigm of the universe is being carefully prepared for your acceptance.

Now comes the great hushed dome itself. At its centre the multi-lensed projector, the altar from which illumination is about to come. Finally there is the darkness and the quiet priestly voice of him who will guide our feet on the celestial journey. One sits in the darkness realizing how fascinating it is to see the timeless devices of religion wedded to this shining sanctuary of science.

As you sit, the marvellous machine lurches and sways in the middle of the building like a great dark beast. It shines its myriad lens on the dome. Effortlessly you are taken on a vast journey. Across the solar system you go, across the galaxy, out across the gulf to the farthest galaxies. You are given a great deal of information, shown diagrams. Courses are plotted for you, planets and stars named, everything neatly placed and catalogued.

Yet a strange thing happens, and I suggest that this strange contradiction is the main glory of a planetarium. The more one is told by that quiet voice, the more information one is given, one finds that the universe is not thereby lessened nor made more manageable. For beyond the facts and theories and discoveries, something more is communicated. That something is awe and wonder. That is why, if you so choose, a planetarium can become a place for worship.

When I look at thy heavens, the work of thy fingers, the moon and the stars which thou hast established; what is man that thou art mindful to him. . . ? Psalm 8:3,4

The Image of God

My friend who is the director of the planetarium was excited. He had been given an invitation to be present in the Jet Propulsion Laboratory in Pasadena to see the first photographs of the planet Saturn come in from the infinitely distant camera of Voyager I.

I want to express a thought about human kind and our place in things. Just suppose you could somehow have hovered in the vicinity of that vast celestial body with its awe inspiring rings, hovering at that point in time which earth calls 11 November 1980. Suddenly, from the direction of the third planet out from the Sun, there appears in the eternal night a tiny shimmering object. Slowly it drifts in and out of the great rings. It circles the giant star, and is then hurled by the planet's gravity across the yawning gulf between Saturn and Jupiter, and so goes travelling on its eternal journey.

As you watch, you see that it is tiny and transient, visible only for a moment. It looks pitiably insignificant against that gargantuan planet and the vast chasm of space. But just suppose that its coming has introduced into this terrible cosmic desert a totally new thing, the mystery we call consciousness. If that is so, then of course its tiny size, its pitiable fragility, its transcience, no longer matter. What matters is its uniqueness.

Maybe the unique contribution to the great cosmic drama which has been made through our human existence is precisely that, consciousness. Medievel men spoke of human kind as possessing what they called "imago dei," the image of God. It is fashionable to question such a concept. It has yet to be proved necessarily wrong. Perhaps the mechanical eye that allows us to see Saturn is only a pale blinkered reflection of a far greater and eternal eye — the eye of God.

. . . *God created man in his own image, male and female he created them.* Genesis 1:27

Faster Than Light

All of us know that humanity is constantly looking around the universe. On the tops of mountains and in lonely places the great telescopes sit and move their slow but very clear eyes about the sky. Today I am here in the planetarium for an hour or two doing a segment of a television program.

As many of us know, we curious humans have developed another extension to our probing out from the planet. From places like Jodrell Bank in England our great technological ears, the antennae of our radio telescopes, send their signals out into the vastness of space. That way we have extended our capacity to see (or should we say to "hear") our way much deeper into space.

Now as we have been doing this, we have always believed that there were certain (not many but a few) unchanging truths in that vast expanse beyond us. One of these "givens" is the speed with which light travels. For some reason it's one of life's statistics that most of us remember. The speed of light is 186,000 miles a second. Think about it and the mind stretches.

But we have always believed that nothing can travel faster than the speed of light. We still do. Yet in the past couple of years that belief has been shaken to the core. For it seems that far far out in the universe, near the edge of our present capacity to probe, there are galaxies whose component parts are moving apart at speeds which are several times the velocity of light! The issue is not yet resolved, and no one knows when it will be. I mention it as something awesome and wondrous, because I think a sense of awe and wonder is very necessary. For awe and wonder are among the elements of life which lead us to worship. There are other things, but awe and wonder are such a way.

The heavens declare the glory of God; and the firmament sheweth his handywork. Psalm 19:1

In Many a Guise

We occupy many rooms. We walk down many corridors. We play many roles. We experience many nuances, and we send many messages. All this we do without ever realizing most of it.

I have just come into this small cramped doctor's waiting room. Stepping over other people's crossed legs I stand at the desk and present the chit given to me by the doctor. It entitles me (if that is the word) to an X-ray in this office. The small dark haired receptionist is bright, cheerful, friendly. The warmth is also in her eyes, where you cannot force it or pretend it. I begin to wait, sliding into a chair, rummaging through the ancient magazines with month old news, which assumes a significance only because one wants to keep the mind occupied.

After a while there comes to the door an elderly man. He is bent, moving very slowly, and is unsure of himself. His face is glum and his eyes downcast. He too goes to the desk. The voice of the receptionist rises as she repeats a greeting and a question. It doesn't sharpen as it rises. There is no impatience. She jokes a little with this man who could be her grandfather. He begins to respond. They chat, and he comes to find a seat among us. I notice that his face is different. There is a risidual smile on it from his encounter with her. His eyes look ahead of him now and are not downcast, as they were when he entered. They move out to meet our eyes. He has emerged. He has been addressed. He has for a moment had his humanity nourished.

This girl would be amazed, perhaps amused, perhaps embarrassed, if I told her that she has a healing gift. But she has.

The virtuous will say to the king, "Lord, when did we see you a stranger and make you welcome?" . . . And the king will answer, "I tell you solemnly, in so far as you did this to one of the least of these . . . , you did it to me." Matthew 25: 37–40

Narcissus

We have know each other off and on for about twenty years. It has been intermittent because we have always worked in widely separate parts of the country. One day recently we got into a long conversation in his office.

I realized that he had made a long interior journey in recent years. Physically he had changed. It was hard to define, but there was a more studied developing of his self-image. Hair was done expensively and styled. Clothes were very fashionable. I had heard that a marriage had come apart.

He wanted to speak of spirituality. He had become deeply involved. There had been retreats in various traditions, Christian as well as eastern. There had been some sessions of self-development. There had been a learning of meditation techniques, and he told me he was now meditating a great deal.

It was all very late twentieth century. In saying this I am not in the least sneering or faultfinding. But somehow there went through everything the sad note of self.

Quite obviously there is great value in going on a spiritual journey. It is very legitimate to try to find oneself. But it seems to me that there is a terribly thin line between self-discovery and self-centredness. The ancients were very wise to put before the discovery of self the discovery of God.

. . . *seek first his kingdom and his righteousness.* . . .
Matthew 6:33

Dilettante

We were discussing a certain couple who are now on the other side of the world. He had known them better than I had. I had seen the surface — pleasant, articulate, sophisticated. I had noticed that from time to time there were periods of some kind of emotional collapse, but the situation would usually right itself, and the outside appearance would again be assumed.

My friend had seen more. As far as he could see, they lived out, or tried to live out, a life style that as much as possible tried to taste everything available. Events, types of friends, fads, trends, attitudes — a whole endless kaleidoscope of trying this and trying that. If TM was fashionable, they tried it. If Est promised self-integration, then they gave it a weekend. If a little mutual sexual freedom seemed the done thing, they tried that. The latest paperback about personal development was beside their bed.

And yet, my friend commented, something almost terrifying seemed to hover in the air as you watched this procession through the endless contempory kaleidoscope. There was a total lack of commitment to any one of these things. In fact, it seemed there was not even an expectation, on their part, that the latest interest would respond more than minimally to the insatiable hunger for changing experience.

I suspect that other societies have offered a fascinating varied spectrum of life styles, interests, behaviour choices. The Mediterranean world around AD 200 did this. Yet many in that world found it was better to make a choice, to commit oneself to a way, to a person, to something calling you to achieve it or serve it or even worship it.

The twentieth century banquet is vast. Some of it is nourishing, some of it is junk, some if it is poisonous. It may seem dull and moralizing to say so, but our choices from the contemporary scene can fulfil us or destroy us.

. . . the time is coming when people . . . will accumulate for themselves teachers to suit their own likings, and will turn away from listening to the truth and wander into myths. 2 Timothy 4:3–6

Highways

Landing Place

The 401 highway in the early morning. Fairly heavy traffic heading east. We have left the city, and the suburbs are flowing by on either side. In these post-snowfall days of January we are moving through a world of black and white and grey. The film of rain on the roadway is drumming on the tires of the car, a distant thunder of wintertime rolling through one's bones. In the distance high apartment towers on a hillside suddenly loom out of the morning fog.

I am driving over a part of the highway that has no buildings beside it. There is a steep bank beyond the shoulder, which slopes off to my right and becomes a green clearing bounded by trees. Up the centre of the field, if one can call it that, there is another deep natural trench. In the summertime the grass there will be long and thick, but now the trench is naked. Bare bushes and branches stick up from it. It is scabrous with patches of dying snow, half dead grass, bare earth.

Suddenly down out of the grey swirling sky swoops a beautiful large bird. The long neck curves, the narrow bill is pointed earthward, the wide wings hold him for a moment as he hovers for landing, his legs ready themselves, and he is down and gone from my sight in the trench. He gives not a glance to that other world beyond his own, the world of concrete and steel, order and system. He inhabits an eternal world of season and cycle, warmth and cold, hunger and appetite.

By a mystery I think him nearer to God than I, in this moment of fleeting morning encounter.

Thou makest springs gush forth in the valleys;. . . By them the birds of the air have their habitation. . . .Psalm 104:10-12

The Ambulance

Literature is full of instances of the moment when a face is seen in a flash and then vanishes. As it does, there may be triggered a poem, a story, a play, a great love that never dies.

I am at a street corner on a Sunday morning. It is still very early, and the world is dutifully observing the Sabbath admonition, at least in the sense of resting. The lights are red and I am waiting. The long empty street on either side tempts me to go. Years of tabu calling for obedience to the law are too strong. I wait. Far down the street there is movement. As yet there is no sound. The distant form quickly becomes a van, the van becomes an ambulance. It is still accelerating as it approaches the lights which now change for me. There is a momentary change in the speed of the ambulance, which then resumes its right-of-way and goes across in front of me.

Suddenly I am aware of a face, a figure sitting beside the driver. She is elderly, her white hair awry after a hasty exit from the house. She is not yet settled in her seat. She is pulling on a cardigan or coat. Her expression is drawn in concern. Others are behind her, unseen in the ambulance.

The face is a haunting one. It bears the universal expression of human anxiety and suffering. It mirrors weariness of what probably has been, fear of what may be, confusion at what is. Seen for a moment, her face stayed in my mind, pale and vulnerable and anxious. Nameless and unknown, I to her and her to me, I yet offer a momentary prayer for her. The lights change again, and I drive on. A little while later I lift her again in the prayers at the altar.

*. . . his faithfulness is a shield and buckler. You will not fear the terrors of the night, nor the arrow that flies by day. . . .*Psalm 91:4,5

The Hands of God

In recent years symbols have come back into modern life after being rather neglected. They were always there lying in wait for our over-rational civilization to rediscover them. There are many reasons for their return. One is the fact that today's large city has such a variety of languages and traditions that words let us down if we depend on them to communicate the same idea to everybody's mind.

Of all contempory institutions it is advertising that has come to realize the necessity for the return of symbols. Ironically the church, rich in symbols, has only recently begun to accept their power again, so mesmerized has Christianity been by ideas and the rational.

That particular thought was triggered by looking to my right as I headed north over a city bridge. There, on top of the brand new Credit Unions building, is a symbol. It wants to say a great deal to me as I dash by. It wants to communicate things like togetherness and caring, security and solidity and dependability. Now those are big words, especially if people dash by as I am doing. So what is put up there on the building? There is a huge pair of bronze-coloured hands holding some symbolic human figures. Incidentally, one of the banks has much the same symbol to remind me with what care and love it is willing to bear me up in any time of need, at of course a considerable rate of interest! But there, high above me, and high above the humdrum of life, are those great symbolic hands.

Here is the supreme irony. Those great hands, symbols of offered monetary security, loom over a society which, in its sad sophistication, is very tempted to dismiss as childish the idea that the truest and deepest way of expressing the love of a creating god is precisely by that same symbol, those same great hands in which the earth, the stars, the very galaxies themselves eternally lie. We are a strange and contradictory civilization.

*Thy hands have made me and fashioned me. . . .*Psalm 119:73

Morning Time

Sunday morning; it is very early. The suburbs are almost totally silent; the trees stand limply in their autumn weariness. The houses huddle in determined sleep, their curtains drawn like great tired eyelids.

I always have a certain guilt as the engine of my little car assumes thunderous power in that Sabbath stillness. I scurry through the streets where sounds seem to ricochet off the houses. I envision bodies heaving over in sleep, bringing down fervent imprecations on my noisy passing. I find myself remembering lines of John Masefield which I learn long years ago in Sixth Form.

> With a struggle for breath the lamp flame fluttered,
> Caesar turned in his bed and muttered
> the house is falling,
> the beaten men come into their own.

I have a vision of my engine making many Caesars (and Calpurnias) turn in their beds and mutter.

Now I am away from the houses. My guilt is lifted. I pass the svelte showrooms of automobiles, and suddenly the misty turrets of the bridge are there, beyond it the highrises above the morning fog. I am in the city now. Staff members coming from the hospital in tired uniforms look for the first coffee of the day — after the last coffee of the night. I go through the streets, empty now that the Saturday night crowds have laid down to sleep. All the loves and lusts and appetites and hungers have melted away. The new day begins.

I am in the lane by the church. The little engine sinks to silence. Sunday begins.

. . . a day in thy courts is better than a thousand elsewhere.
Psalm 84:10

Non-Communication

The other day I came out to the lane and found on the window of my car a pamphlet. It was badly printed, lurid, shrill, and arrogant. It wallowed in the contemplation of the evil of human nature. It was loaded with words like *sin, guilt, punishment,* giving them huge capital letters. It was peppered with biblical quotations. When you have read the first shrieking paragraph you can fill in the rest. I am sure that you have come across the kind of thing I am talking about.

I suppose what makes me most sad and, if I am honest, most mad at this sort of thing, is that it is done by people who, I am quite sure, would not only claim to be Christian, but would claim it with the same angry passion that this grimy piece of paper speaks it. Above all else, what strikes me as most tragic is how this approach to other human beings is so totally opposite from the approach of the person in whose name it is all done.

If I can presume to say anything about Jesus of Nazareth, I am certain that he would not, if only because he never did, develop a kind of hit and run approach to people. Everything he did and said presumes the context of a relationship.

I suppose that the most ironic thing about the kind of person who puts a pamphlet on my windshield telling me that, if I don't cease immediately to be a consummate sinner and believe every single word in the Bible, I shall go straight to hell, is this — whether they realize it or not, they are projecting onto me and others the hell of fear and anxiety and alienation that blazes away inside themselves.

Who shall bring any charge against God's elect? It is God who justifies; who is to condemn? Romans 8:33,34

The Star

I am thirty thousand feet over the Rockies, flying west for home. I say that we are over the mountains instinctively rather than from any evidence. At this early dawn hour, about 6:25 in the morning, we are moving over a pitch black ocean of cloud that still waits for a morning sun to give it form.

The distant line of division between the horizon of clouds and the upper sky is starkly drawn. Here, on the line of deepest darkness, the emerging light is brightest to the southeast. As you look upward, the light changes, band after band and shade after shade moves through a spectrum of darkening blue until, high in the arch of the heavens, there is still darkness. There, like a great jewel set out meticulously for display against a cloth of black velvet, the star hangs.

It is absolutely alone in the morning sky. It hangs strong and clear, defying the coming of the sun for a new day. I suppose it is this time of year that makes me think of another star hanging over another darkened terrain in another long-ago world. I link that long-ago time with this personal epiphany given to me in this early dawn moment of my later century. I recall how these ancient travellers journeyed, following their conviction that there would somewhere be a birth. Were they wise men because they searched, or did they search because they were wise? I suppose it was partly both.

Our anxious and fractious history very badly needs a star. Later, as I still write, the sky is brighter, but the star still blazes undiminished.

The light shines in the darkness, and the darkness has not overcome it. John 1:5

Niagara

As you cross Lake Ontario, flying the last leg of a flight from the United States into Canada, very frequently the pilot will say that he is going to make a bit of a detour so that people can look down on Niagara Falls. The plane banks slightly and swings to the West. Down below, the grey-blue water shimmers under the morning sun; a small craft draws the line of its wake as a child might draw a chalk mark on a vast grey slate; the wake, as the chalk mark, is swiftly eradicated. In the plane, people begin to move toward the left side, sliding into vacant seats or craning apologetically over other shoulders. Far below there is the familiar pattern of the river, sweeping the eye toward the cauldron half hidden by the spray, then on down the gorge until the flood escapes into the waiting expanse of the lake.

No great offering of nature could be more surrounded and smothered by our human debris than Niagara. From it's edge there sweep back in circles the legions of our exploitative humanity — shops, booths, concessions, offices, hotels, motels, restaurants, theatres, video arcades. Millions of times a day the terror and power of Niagara are imprisoned in Kodak slides. What more can we do to make it a vast prisoner for our greed and pleasure!

Yet the majesty remains, the thunderous voice is undiminished, the vast crown of sun drenched spray is borne by Niagara most royally. Maybe even our worst cannot despoil the world.

The earth is the Lord's and the fullness thereof . . . . Psalm 24:1

The Choice

The flight was half empty. It was also the first flight of a Sunday, and it was very early in the morning. Things were quiet and leisurely. The meal had been served, and there was still some time before getting ready for the final approach to the runway. The cabin crew were feeling relaxed.

Near to me there was a baby. The young mother was alone; so one of the crew took the baby for a while and began to play. The child was at that stage of being able, in a very early way, to dialogue. It smiled, crinkled up its eyes, reached about with its hands for that adult face, and puckered the skin with its tiny fingers, just learning their own strength. For quite a long time the hostess played with him, and it was only when the signal came for the last minute things to be done before the flight ended, that she gave him back to his mother.

None of that is remarkable in any way. But it was about ten minutes later that the usual sounds of tidying up the galley were going on and there was a conversation. I overheard the voice saying, "Of course, if you had a child, you would have to give up a lot of other things."

I couldn't help feeling how that single sentence hanging in mid-air from a conversation between two women sums up the dilemma that faces many women, as the horizons of choice and freedom broaden. It also occurred to me that, difficult though the choice may be, at least when it is taken for motherhood, then, because it is a conscious choice, it is all the more likely to be carried out fulfillingly and well.

Teach me thy way, O Lord, that I may walk in thy truth. . . .
Psalm 86:11

Music From Afar

I am sitting in this aisle seat on the early morning flight east. Before I begin to do some work, I pick up the headset and finger the dial around to the classical band. As the tape begins, the announcer's voice lists the program items. There is a mention of Beethoven and Mozart who, wonderful though they may be, are of course names distant in time. They have become their music and are really no longer persons to us.

Then I hear the name of an old friend, not long dead, who has given much lovely music to Canada. The piece was called "Divertimento for Organ and two Oboes," by Robert Fleming. As I listened, there was a face and a voice and a smile, and eyes and movements remembered. I found that I was receiving a friend's gift across the immeasurable gulf of life and death. And I was moved to think that perhaps that much dreaded gulf is considerably narrower than we suspect. At such moments it seems so.

The fact that I was receiving a gift of beauty and creativity, from a friend now in that state which we call death, made me think again of the mysterious line between those of us who live and those of us who — what shall we say — do not live? What does it mean to say that?

The music, to which I am listening at this moment, is as much Robert now as it was when he heard it from beyond himself, and felt it come through him onto paper and keyboard. Therein lies perhaps the most haunting thought — what links us all across the gulf is the source of the music itself. Because of that source the music is neither his nor mine, but it and he and I and all of us are possessed by that same source whose name is God.

. . . whether we live . . . or whether we die, . . . we are the Lord's.
Romans 14:8

A Sleeping Giant

We met as we pulled down the overhead baggage rack to put in our coats. Each of us then went through all the traditional ceremonies that humans perform when they realize they will be sitting cheek by jowl for four hours in a plane, and they have not yet decided whether they even want to acknowledge each other's existence. As it happened the flight was delayed; so we naturally had to share that one human feeling that cannot be fully savoured in silence or alone — exasperation. That of course broke the ice and led to other things.

He informed me of his numerous encounters with officialdom and with institutions, encounters from which he invariably emerged as the victor. I was flying with an unknown and unsung Ralph Nader. He informed me of the importance and comparative uniqueness of what he did for a living. He outlined an itinerary of reponsibility in which his advent at various branches of his business would put, so I understood, nervous colleagues on their mettle until he flew further on his journey.

He had a couple of pleasant drinks and an equally pleasant dinner, and the scene changed. There had been some family life, and now it was gone. In a large city there was an apartment which was comfortable and near the office and fairly expensive and horribly empty.

Eventually he went to sleep. While he slept, the authority melted away; his jawline changed and the smooth severity of hair became tousled. He slept — a rather tired, lonely, and vulnerable human being from whom weariness had taken the mask he was so determined to wear. So it is with you and with me and with all of us.

Thou knowest when I sit down and when I rise up; thou discernest my thoughts from afar. Psalm 139:2

The Wise Man

The obvious fact that it is a changing world is communicated in various ways, sometimes brutally and depressingly, but sometimes in terms of hope and possibility.

A doctor once said to me that if you are going to sit in an aeroplane for three or four hours, you should get up every hour and walk the length of the plane. Just to make an idle observation, planes these days are getting long enought to let one have a reasonable walk. Also, I am glad that everyone's doctor has not given them this advice because then the aisles would be very crowded!

On my first walk I noticed him. I don't really know why. I didn't know him. I suppose it was because he looked a classic type. He sat in a sea of darkness because the movie was on in the cabin. In his personal pool of light he had his mobile office arranged. From the briefcase there spilled papers. There was a calculator at hand, some paper clips, pens. Oblivious to the siren shadows of the movie, he worked.

Time passed by, and I went for my second walk. As I approached, I noticed again how he sat in a solitary non-conforming pool of light. But this time the office accoutrements had gone. Briefcase, calculator, paper clips, pens had all vanished. He sat reading. I could see what he was reading. It was called *The Palace of Nowhere*, a book by a Trappist monk who knew Thomas Merton in the monastery at Gethsemane in Kentucky. It's a deep and lovely series of spiritual meditations.

The world is changing. I couldn't help thinking that, for at least one man, it was perfectly rational to bring into a balanced whole his exterior and interior lives. It was very good to meet a wise man.

. . . they that wait upon the Lord shall renew their strength; they shall mount up with wings as eagles; they shall run and not be weary; and they shall walk, and not faint. Isaiah 40:31

The Prisoner

I was walking down the hallway to the room for boarding the flight, and I had stopped a moment to make a telephone call. As I did so, I noticed the three men. Something about them made me look a second time, and I noticed that two of them were handcuffed together.

Now you might say that there is nothing strange about that, and there isn't. But there is something about such a sight that makes you think a lot about this fragile thing we call our humanity.

Why was it immediately obvious to me which man was prisoner? All three were about the same age. I watched after they had passed and couldn't help noticing how diminished a man is by being a prisoner. Captivity droops the body. I noticed that while two of the men talked animatedly, the third not only remained silent but seemed somehow not to exist for the others. He could have been a piece of baggage handcuffed to a human wrist in case of robbery. The eyes of the free men were alive. They moved around with that normal awareness of the passing scene which we all have. But the eyes of the prisoner were dead. They looked into the near distance as if he had surrounded himself with a personal shield in which he moved among the rest of us yet remained strangely in another reality or another time.

Later I saw them again as they left the plane elsewhere in the province. The hostess gave her statutory smile to the two men. From the third man her eyes slid away, and he did not try to engage them.

I know captivity is a normal thing in our society. It is also often a necessary thing. But that does not change the fact that it is a very terrible thing.

The virtuous will say to the king, "Lord when did we see you in prison and go to see you? And the king will answer, "I tell you solemnly, in so far as you did this, to one of the least of these, you did it to me." Matthew 25: 37–40

Midnight At The Airport

It's a few minutes to midnight. The airport is quiet. Half the restaurant area is closed. The magazine and drug store windows are dark. At the check-ins only a few people are on duty. It's that hour when even airports lose their doubtful glamour and the human face has a certain greyness of skin. Any who are travelling do so because they have to.

I am standing at the entrance to the security check. In front of me is a young man, short and stocky, putting a heavy bag on the belt of the X-ray machine. With his other arm he is holding a very young child, an infant. I take no particular notice, until beside me the voice of a woman says to the security checker, "Don't take the bag. Don't let him on the plane." The security person takes refuge in officialdom. She says that if he has a ticket he must be allowed through. "If you do," the young woman says, "you'll be helping him to kidnap my child."

For a moment she reaches out for the child. The young man pulls away from her and rushes through the security check, grasping the child, his face a mask of sadness, anger, exhaustion. Beside me equally drawn and mask-like, the girl turns to search for police. Later I see him being questioned quietly in the corner. He is eventually allowed to travel.

You and I read about it so often. It's commonplace. A relationship arrives at a blank wall. Love turns to hate. Communications break down. But to see it at midnight, to see the tears and to hear the voices and to sense a total desperation — to be a witness to it makes you realize that no human agony is ever commonplace.

O Lord make haste to help me! Let them be put to shame and confusion altogether who seek to snatch away my life. . . .Psalm 40:14

Airport Goodbye

It isn't for nothing that we say that eyes are the windows of the soul.

I am at that point in all airports where those who are travelling must now separate themselves from those who are not. Depending on the circumstances, the relationship, or the duration of the separation, people behave here in all sorts of different ways. The wives of busy executives receive or give the requisite peck on the departing cheek and turn untroubled toward the exit. Small children are handed uncomprehendingly from one set of arms to another to be kissed.

As I move through the gate toward the security check, she moves back from the door, a goodbye just said to someone unseen. She is in, I would say, her late fifties, early sixties. Our eyes meet for a second as she turns from the task of farewell. All sorts ot things are there, as if images registered intensely have not yet faded when she begins already to receive new ones. The goodbye has been costly. Her eyes say that more subtly than weeping — which she is not. It is the look of someone who has deliberately not wept so that someone else can be spared. In the same second she is already determinedly dealing with the moment of farewell, placing it firmly under "items accomplished" and not to be lingered over. There are things to be done. A cup of coffee perhaps. Finding the car in the parking lot. Getting home in the afternoon traffic. Maybe then letting go. Maybe, maybe not. Wordsworth once spoke of "the still sad music of humanity."

. . . *I die daily.* 1 Corinthians 31

Outdoors

The Tree

The conference I had to attend was an interesting one. There came a time when it broke up into groups. On such a beautiful day it was suggested we could hold the groups outside. In our group I was the first to find a spot. It was on the grass under a great tree. Then I did something that I haven't done for a long time. The others had not yet arrived; so I lay on my back on the grass and just looked up into the tree.

For thousands, tens of thousands of years, trees were thought of as sacred. When I was a child, there was on the farm a grove of trees that had something special about it. I was never sure why it was different, but it was. And even when in later years a golf links was made on that land, the grove of trees was allowed to remain. I suspect that, for a thousand years before me on that hillside, other children and other adults had regarded the grove as — let's use the real word — *sacred*.

As I lay on the ground, I realized again why a tree is capable of filling a human being with a sense of awe. As I looked up into its spreading branches and leaves, I realized that I was looking into the depths of a many-layered world, something that was almost a little universe in itself. There were openings visible between branches, like doors tantalizingly leading into other rooms, other paths, other galleries — almost like a vast labyrinth.

If so, was there a central room? Was there a central holy place, a heart to this living world where, if my eyes could penetrate, I would see the One who dwelled there and was King, and to whom I would bow down and worship? So in that moment under the beauty of the tree, I offered worship to Him who made it.

. . . the tree of life also in the midst of the garden. . . . Genesis 2:9

Sunset

It was an hour of great beauty, the kind of beauty that the ocean and the coast give frequently. Toward the coming of evening the sun settles on the waters of the gulf, seeming to delay its setting, to pour itself along the waters. Reaching the city it transforms the apartment buildings into vast reflectors that flash and ripple as the angle of the sun slowly changes.

We were walking in the area of the museum, watching the sailing craft head home after the day. Here and there the occasional working craft was coming in — tug boats, a police patrol boat. As we walked, we turned around a headland and were then facing westward out toward the late evening sun.

I became aware that others at various points around us were likewise looking out. They were not talking to each other, not even looking at one another, although they were obviously there together. Almost all were facing west, almost all were still and silent.

What came to me has been expressed best by the late C.S. Lewis. He occupied the chair of English at Cambridge and was a very famous convert to Christianity. He would say that we humans are all really exiles from another reality which some call heaven. In our exile we are given glimpses of a loveliness and a glory which are our true surroundings. For we are haunted by a music and a dancing and a language we once spoke but have forgotten. Lewis had a word for this. He called it joy. He often emphasized that he did not mean happiness necessarily, certainly not mere jollity. He was referring to a longing, a longing for something you know with absolute certainty to be real and of infinite value but which cannot, at least in the present moment, be fully possessed. For Lewis that something was the divine glory which is at the heart of things.

As we stood facing the gulf, I was aware of being granted a fleeting moment of that joy.

> *O world invisible*
> *We view thee.*
> *O work intangible*
> *We touch thee.*

Francis Thompson

A Child's Insight

There is an old phrase that I have quoted beneath this passage. It is a verse from one of the ancient Jewish psalms. The expression "out of the mouths of babes" is often used to comment on a statement made sometimes by a child who unwittingly "hits the nail on the head."

I couldn't help overhearing two small voices discussing the sun. After a few preliminary remarks one small voice said, "And you know, it's very big and it's awful hot, and God made it." There was a moment's silence as they both considered this observation. Then the other small voice said, "Yes, he did, and you know something, he isn't finished yet."

It is so fascinating to hear a child utter an insight into the nature of God which many adults never fully realize. For centuries millions of people read the opening chapters of the Book of Genesis and were taught from it that the universe is the creation of God. But it became for most people something that took place away back in the dawn of time, an event locked away in the ancient pages of an ancient book.

For a period, ironically called the Enlightenment, there was made popular in the philosophy of the age an image of God as the great watchmaker. He had set the created order going. Essentially it was now finished. He merely watched its operation, and some said, while others vehemently denied, he stepped in from time to time to interfere with the workings.

Yet the Judeo-Christian concept of God says that the process of creation is not a single event in a long-ago past. Creation is an endless heaving ocean of life forming and growing and changing, dying and coming again to birth in ways beyond our imagining. The grandeur of the concept challenges the greatest human minds. Yet I overhear it expressed clearly and succinctly in the lisping words of a small child.

> *Thine is the kingdom,*
> *the power, and the glory,*
> *for ever and ever. Amen.*

Child of Summer

At a certain time of the year, when the very last garments of winter have vanished and we have even looked awhile on the lovely face of springtime, we begin to long for summertime. Because we are human, we exercise a little excusable self-deception. It gives us the delicious and pathetic delusion that we are the masters and mistresses of time. We take our clocks, and we put them on one hour.

It has no devastating effect on life. There is the slight adjustment to the first morning which seems to come with depressing haste. In the little world of parish churches there is the inevitable few who forgot the hour and arrive earlier than they have done in six months, sheepishly acknowledging their mistake.

But there is one great and important change we make in the world by moving our clocks ahead to summer time. It is a change easily missed, yet once realized you are always aware of it again.

It is 7.30 in the evening. The light is gentle, the trees and the grass along the street are drying after the day's showers. The street is familiar yet different. There is a sound I don't associate with leaving the house for an evening meeting. Then I see them farthur up the street. They are playing in the last hour of the day's sunlight. With them is the dog, almost as large as they are. They are discovering a new time called evening, a new miracle called sunset. They are the children of a new summertime. They are the renewing of the world.

For you are all children of light and children of the day; we are not of the night or of darkness. 1 Thessalonians 5:5

The Sea Shepherd

Blue sky and blazing sun, morning in the city, the silence of early Sunday hours. I leave the altar of the cathedral and take off the vestments of Eucharist, pick up a prayer book and a white stole, and get into the car. Down toward the harbour, east along the dockside streets, left across the railway tracks, through the warehouses and parking lots and docks; suddenly I have arrived.

They are waiting, about thirty of them. They are all younger than I. Because of the tide the deck of the ship is below the level of the dock. It is a twenty-year-old former North Sea trawler. We go down the steep gangway and make a circle on the rear deck. In the next few minutess, we express some simple things. I read some verses of the first chapter of Genesis, the great and majestic song of creation. Incidentally in that song I notice that the only creature in all of God's creation specifically mentioned by name is the great whale. I mention that fact because to these gallant people that creature is their absolute commitment. It is a commitment so high that it could conceivably demand their lives.

We say two prayers which express thanks and an asking of God for a sense of responsibility for the created order. Then all the men and women in silence exchange a handshake or embrace of peace. There follows a simple blessing, and we say goodbye.

Sometime the next day the Sea Shepherd headed out under the bridge. The ship is for many reasons a political "hot potato." But the men and the women on it are ready to risk their lives for a great and lovely creature pursued by a Russian whaling fleet. Before doing that they asked for a prayer and a blessing. I felt that they should be given it.

Yonder is the sea, great and wide, which teems with things innumerable. . . . .There go the ships and Leviathan which thou didst form to sport in it. Psalm 104:25,26

Dandelion

Sometimes at evening and sometimes in the morning, I do my modest jogging. I do it on a high school track, which gives me an easy method of knowing how much I have done.

I was going around the outside track, letting my mind wander as it would. I gradually became aware of the white round globes that dandelions become when they go to seed. All along the edge they hung out over the track, brushing against my ankles as I passed. Instinctively I moved out a little so as not to hit them. I found myself remembering a small child in another far away field and in another autumn, plucking dandelions, blowing them, and saying with each blow, "One o'clock, two o'clock, three o'clock," and seeing how long in the sequence of the hours the seeds would last as they blew away from the stem.

When I drew to a puffing halt at the end of the jog and had walked a little, I plucked a dandelion. I looked at it closely and saw a dark heart, the seeds on tiny stems forming a delicate complex sphere. The child in me blew at it. As I did so, the adult in me noticed how the heart of the sphere became white as if, the seeds and the stems gone, it had bled and so perished.

As I let it drop on the grass I realized something eternal. It came to me that even as the broken green stem lay on the ground, its white head waiting for the coming of winter, it had already sent on the evening air those seeds that would give life to the springtime for which the whole world would long.

. . . *if God so clothe the grass of the field, which today is alive and tomorrow is thrown into the oven, will he not much more clothe you, O men of little faith?* Matthew 6:30

Staying Power

I was chatting to someone who had been through a really rough time. We had spoken abouth the days of struggle and the nights of sleeplessness. It doesn't matter what the reason was, because there are ten thousand reasons why life becomes rough.

In the course of conversation he mentioned a particular episode. In one sense it may seem to you to be very everyday and ordinary. On reflection I think you will find it worth a great deal.

He told me that there was a day when he had to leave the office. He just couldn't take it, and he left to be anywhere other than there. He found himself walking out on one of the city beaches, crushed by depression and hopelessness. Gradually he became aware of a tugboat hauling a huge log boom out on the bay. He noticed how it moved so slowly; in fact, it was almost stationary, but it did move! In the stillness across the water he began to hear, and in a sense to feel deeply within himself, the sound of that great hidden engine. He told me that somehow it entered into him and became a kind of sign or word, a response to his pain. After a while he turned away and returned into the city. He found that somehow he had been given the power to move in the face of all that had been crushing his capacity to live. In the beating of his heart he heard a sound deeper and greater.

Just an ordinary tugboat, but then God is always using the most appallingly ordinary things to speak to us.

Whither shall I go from thy Spirit? If I . . . dwell in the uttermost parts of the sea, even there thy hand shall lead me. Psalm 139: 9,10

Arctic Evening

There were, I think, five of us in the group, and we were trying to do something difficult, difficult in the sense that it would be easy to do it badly. We were trying to put into words a moment or an incident in our lives when we were very aware of that mystery or "otherness" or presence which most of the time we are unaware of, because of busyness and activity. One such moment I want to share.

It doesn't matter what his name is. For years he has lived and worked in both the eastern and western Arctic as a priest. He is fluent in its dialects. As much as it ever can be for one not born there, it is his land and his home and his people.

"A couple of years ago," he told us, "I set out to visit a group of hunters who were about ten days travel away. When I got to them, they were preparing to turn for home again. So I journeyed back with them. The weather was a series of perfect Arctic days for travelling. Hour after hour we sped along. There were eight teams of dogs; there were children and parents. And the bells sounded and the children called to one another and the dogs barked and we raced mile after mile across the white world.

"There came an evening when we camped, and I walked away across a little rise by myself. When I came back, I suddenly became aware of something very unusual in an Inuit camp. Just for a moment the camp lay before me; people were moving about. But for that moment no dog barked and no child cried out. There was no wind. Only complete silence. For that moment I became aware in a new way of the ancient words, 'The Peace of God which passeth all understanding'." All of us have moments like that, if only we recognize them.

The peace of God which passeth all understanding, shall keep your hearts and minds through Christ Jesus. Philippians 4:7

April

An early spring day on the west coast, about noon. I am driving south-west from the city and up the long incline that eventually sweeps around and dives into the tunnel under the river. Here the traffic picks up speed. Each of us roars along in our steel enclave, the mingling of the engine and tyres and radio or tape creating the sound that has become at times the unconscious background to our lives.

I suppose I notice them because of their sudden joyous movements. They are away on the edge of vision, yet in spite of the demands of traffic on one's attention, I cannot help but glance a number of times. They are in the field next to the road. Some lie on the grass in the shadow of the mother sheep. Others are moving with that sudden ecstatic skipping of their kind. They are the newly born lambs of Spring.

I am immediately aware of them on many levels. I am aware that fifty yards away is the absolute opposite of this roaring world of steel and concrete through which I race. Over there is the slow, eternal, almost silent cycle of nature, framed in the noonday sunlight. I find myself recalling a lovely thing learnt long ago in a parish schoolhouse.

> All in the April evening,
> April airs were abroad,
> The sheep with their little lambs
> passed me by on the road.
>
> The sheep with their little lambs
> passed me by on the road,
> all in the April evening
> I thought on the lamb of God.

For centuries the image of the lamb has for Christians linked the divine and the human. I drove on once again, aware of how infinitely rich are the great images and symbols of the faith we have inherited.

. . . the lamb in the midst of the throne will be their shepherd. Rev. 7:17

Other Books by Herbert O'Driscoll

One Man's Journal
160 pages, paper

Spiritual reflections on contemporary living selected from six years of daily radio talks on stations CHQM, CKOR, CKXR in British Columbia. Seeing with the author's eyes, we discover the eternal dimensions in people, places, and current events.

"On the air or in print, Herbert O'Driscoll is a rarity among theologians. He communicates to the lay person with clarity, humour, and insight" — Roy Bonisteel, *CBC TV, Man Alive.*

"These many facets of O'Driscoll's imaginative mind convey a light-heartedness which is good medicine for an uncertain age" — *Algoma Anglican.*

"One of the best preachers in the English-speaking world today' — *Presbyterian Record.*

Crossroads
Times of decision for the people of God
96 pages, paper

How can we face crucial decisions? Which way should we turn? Herbert O'Driscoll enters the times and lives of Moses, St Paul, Thomas Becket, Archbishop Romero, and others, discovering the presence of God in moments of crisis, and giving us courage to meet our own crossroads. A quotation from scripture, an historical overview, and a dramatic reconstruction draw us inexorably into each situation, and allow the spiritual experiences of others to enlighten our lives.

Portrait of a Woman
Meditations of the Mother of our Lord
96 pages, paper

Renowned author, journalist, and broadcaster, Herbert O'Driscoll
has produced a beautifully and sensitively drawn portrait of the
Virgin Mary in the form of a series of short meditations on selected
passages of Scripture.

"Feminists, Protestants, and those not familiar with Catholic tradition, will be intrigued to 'get inside' Mary through this poetic and
imaginative narrative. Herbert O'Driscoll, by painting an engaging
portrait of Mary's *inward* journey and the feelings she 'could have
had' for Jesus, invites us to contemplate the mystery of love and
suffering" — Lois M. Wilson, *Moderator, United Church of
Canada.*

A Certain Life
Contemporary Meditations on the Way of Christ
96 pages, paper

Through the artistry of Herbert O'Driscoll, we enter the life and
time of Jesus and his disciples, and return again across the years to
our present time, refreshed with a new understanding and a clearer
vision of life. Now in its second printing.

For All Seasons
A Devotional Commentary on the Prayer Book Lectionary
160 pages, paper

Superb starting points for sermons or meditations. With a light
touch and penetrating vision, Herbert O'Driscoll cogently relates
Prayer Book scripture and teaching on current attitudes and situa-
tions.

"An exciting example of true Bible exposition. In clear, lucid
language, O'Driscoll takes us right to the heart of the collect, epis-
tle, and gospel for each Sunday of the Church Year" — Leonard
Griffith.

The Unshakable Kingdom
125 pages, paper

A dynamic vision of human redemption in the face of global catastrophe. Herbert O'Driscoll hears the voice of God in the contemporary "whirlwind" — business and commerce, sexuality and relationships, physical science and technology, psychology and the journey of the soul — and he proclaims hope to a listening church.

"The book will be useful to the enquirer who needs a fresh presentation of what Christianity has to offer him; to the preacher who wants to hear the message proclaimed by a master communicator, and to the regular churchgoer who enjoys having his faith stirred up, challenged, and reinforced all at the same time" — John Baycroft